Set Dance Speed

90 MPH

AN IRISH DANCE NOVELLA

MEGH DEVLIN

For all the dancers in my life: may all your days be sparkly.

Author's Note

In the interest of unity in the Irish dance world, the author chose against modelling the Oireachtas of the novella after the Oireachtas of any particular dancing organization. For this reason, dancing levels, the time of year that this Oireachtas takes place in, or various rules mentioned throughout are a deliberate mash-up of many organizations. It is the author's hope that all dancers can see their story being told through Elodie's voice.

Thank-you, and happy reading

Chapter 1

"You need to work HARDER." Mr. Declan is shouting, and not for the first time tonight.

Róisín and I are both gasping our way through our hornpipe but I know Mr. Declan is mostly talking to me. I don't think I've heard him give Róisín anything more than a suggestion since she was sixteen and won third place at Worlds.

My quads are burning. I can feel the rawness of my toe knuckles as I hop-- en pointe! en pointe! en pointe! My ankles wobble with fatigue, a hairline from a fracture if I were to fall out of my tall stance.

"Four more counts! Suck it up!"

I can't begin to explain the feeling of a third hornpipe step. It's like my legs have been buried halfway in sand and are being knocked around by red flag riptides. Limp, wet reeds dangle from my hips.

I click through into one of the weakest overs of my life. I stumble a bit and bang into into Róisín's shoulder by mistake but she does not miss a beat.

"And treble hop BACK and duh da da duh!"

We hold the pose, our left toe cocked daintily in front of the right. I don't know about Ro, but I feel like my lungs are about the size of dimes for all the air I seem to be getting.

"Ladies, what's the breathing about?"

We glance at each other, forcing ourselves to swallow burning air.

Róisín speaks up. "St-stamina sucks."

I let out a shocked giggle.

Mr. Declan cracks a grin. "Sure does."

However, there is some approval. "Your diddly squats weren't the worst I've seen them. Get a drink. Let's see if I can be more impressed by the next pair."

Ah, a compliment. If only they were all so easy to come by.

Introductions in the Irish dance world go something like this:

My name is Elodie Kennedy; I am 19 and dance for the Rooney Academy of Irish Dance. I have been in open champs for about a year. My dress is my first and only solo dress and I sometimes think I love it as equally as I love my dog. I don't usually wear a wig but I love a good fake tan.

I have never qualified for the Worlds.

Róisín and I collapse in the farthest corner from our teacher. She immediately pulls off her shoes, wiggling her toes in an attempt to get the circulation going again. She has just bought new ones, again. Every five weeks or so, Róisín will suddenly appear in class with a stiff, shiny new pair of heavies on her feet, still smelling of fresh leather. She won't explain and so I've concluded that she's in some sort of fight club, with heavies as the prize. With hard shoes costing about 150 dollars a pop, it's the only thing that makes sense.

Myself, on the other hand ... I frown woefully at my feet. I have a pair of carefully broken-in competition shoes, but my practice shoes are horrific. The leather is so worn in spots that it has turned gray, and my right heel is held on with gorilla glue. They are so loose that I have to duct tape them to my feet.

I can't hide my jealousy from Róisín. "Tell me, where did you get them? Let me be a part of Heavy Club! Mine are falling to pieces!"

Róisín is impish as she gently places her shining shoes into her dance bag.

"If there were a Heavy Club, which there *isn't,*" she says pointedly, making me scowl. "The first rule would obviously be--"

"Not to talk about Heavy Club," I finish for her. "Obviously you're just afraid I'll beat you up with these fists of fury."

I mime like I'm throwing a dozen punches.

Ro simply laughs and rolls her eyes and begins to lace up her soft shoes in a complicated new pattern.

"Fine then," I say, rummaging through my bag for my soft shoes. I find a bruised banana, three crushed water bottles, and a tube of Icy Hot. "There's no Heavy Club. Are you holding up vendors with a fistful of medals, like homemade brass knuckles? Now that I think of it, I haven't seen that Trading Taps lady in a few months …"

"Actually I told Laura Daly's grandma that I've been searching for years for my long lost Donegal relations and isn't the internet amazing! I've discovered that we're fourth cousins. Then I mentioned the bad state of my shoes and next thing I was on to Tara Shaughnessy's nanny. Who do you think I should go after next?"

I laugh and shove her.

"Shut up! You're such a liar." I giggle.

We get into a small tussle that mostly involves throwing Band-Aid wrappers at each other before Mr. Declan breaks it up.

He shouts, "I've said twice already that I want ye all up for six minutes of threes. But as you ladies have chosen to ignore me, I've decided to make it seven."

I grimace at my hard shoes, still firmly tied, buckled, and taped, then shift my unhappy look to Declan.

Make it eight," I say.

The other ten girls in class groan in unison. Various whines of "Elodie!" and several pouts are hurled in my direction. I find my shoes in my sweatshirt pocket and immediately I begin trying to do the quickest shoe change of my life.

"Finish in thirty seconds and I'll settle for nine," he replies with an extremely pleased grin. TCs love opportunities to torture. Sometimes I'm convinced TC actually stands for Torturer in Command.

I finish my shoe change in record time. I shout, "done!" as I leap to my feet.

Declan snaps his fingers in a low swoop, evidently disappointed at a missed opportunity. "I thought I was going to have a chance to make it ten, Miss Kennedy! Haven't done that in a while."

Okay, so maybe just my TC. Mr. Declan is my uncle by marriage, having married my dad's sister, but I've never caught a break because of it.

I scuttle into line behind one of the serious-seventeens, Kate. Serious-seventeens are what Ro and I call the ones who have realized that they might be nearing the end of their dance career, as high school graduation looms ever closer, and thus put their all and everything into winning.

"Elodie," Kate whispers. "If we're not dead at the end of these ten minutes I'll kill you myself."

She smiles sweetly over her shoulder at me then slides her foot into point. Her arch is gorgeous. In fact, I would have noticed before if she had such great arches, even just standing...

Suddenly, I gasp, scandalized. "You have new shoes, too? Whose second cousin twice removed are you!"

"5-6, and off you go!" Mr. Declan cries, slapping his thigh.

Startled, I start on my left foot and chase after the flowing stream of girls in front of me.

I see Kate's pursed lips, holding back giggles, as we round the corner.

"Mr. Declan," I shout as I glide across the floor. "I think there's an illegal shoe ring! It needs to be stopped!"

Mr. Declan sits in a director's chair, which is labelled *múinteoir*, or teacher, by the stereo. His arms are folded on his chest and he is wearing matching black tracksuit set and a smirk; these are his most defining features, secondary to his blue eyes and short, dark hair.

"Nah," he says seriously. "I gave them the new shoes. I give them to all my favorites. Haven't you heard about the rampant politics in the Irish dance world?"

I know he is joking but I actually am in part really baffled as to where all these new shoes have been coming from; as mentioned, they aren't cheap. I choose indignant as my response as I round the floor a second time.

"Mr. Declan!" I say. "You evil politician!"

I don't know if you know this, but doing threes for any amount of time at speed 113 while laughing is near impossible. However, it is admittedly an excellent core workout.

Mr. Declan shrugs. "Ah well what can I say, I favor those who don't bleed through their socks."

I'm confused as I glance down and suddenly realize that the heels of my white poodle socks are drenched in red. "Oh."

"Watch the turn-out on that back foot, pet," he says. But he does not shout and he throws in a kind wink.

Maybe TC doesn't stand for Torturer in Command.

"Sarah, so help me if you don't kick that bum I will kick it for you!"

Or, at the very least, there are lapses in the meaning.

Róisín and I thank Mr. Declan for class and he reminds us about extra class tomorrow. With that, we haphazardly toss shoes and water bottles into our bags and toss on some sweatpants and sweaters for our walk home.

As we stroll, Ro frowns at me. "Why in the world wouldn't you say anything about those blisters, El?"

Although Róisín won't let me know who her shoe dealer is, she really is my best friend. We have been in class together since day one and Róisín being slightly older and lacking in little siblings to mother, she chose me.

I was four, likely wearing overalls, my dark hair in ballerina-wannabe-bun and probably wouldn't shut up about the packages my Irish nana sent me. In one brown paper parcel had come true love in the form of a Lord of the Dance VHS. I used to watch it twice a day, every day, once before kindergarten and once after, though sometimes I could beg a third viewing before bed, and was I certain that someday I was going to turn into "the princess dancer" AKA Saoirse, Bernadette Flynn.

In fact, if there's one thing that I remember from my first class it is that I kept telling Miss Orla, Mr. Declan's mother, that my name was Saoirse (which, as you can imagine, I could hardly pronounce at age four). My mom was highly embarrassed at my being so difficult and corrected my corrections of my name at every turn. But as Miss Orla shooed her and the other nervous mothers out the door, Róisín took my hand, said she would call me Saoirse, if I'd like, but maybe let my mom call me Elodie, if that's what she liked. Róisín was smart and had the most lovely fluff of curls on her head I had ever seen, not to mention perfect posture at age five and a half, which was very valuable in sticker and Starburst currency of little beginner Irish dance.

As we grew up from first feis-ers to primaries to intermediates, I learned that Ro was never afraid of anything: not hard work or scary teachers or losing or mean girls. With Róisín holding my hand, whether it was in line on my first day of dancing class or onstage waiting for results, I could almost be tricked into believing I was not scared either.

Except sometimes, Ro's mothering scares me, just a teensy bit. She's in her fourth year of studying to be a physical therapist and she has all sorts of expensive books. Books with horror stories of what happens to athletes who forgot about the tiny little ligaments and bones and muscles that make their bodies do athletic-y things and while aching bones might make me worry myself at night, come class time, the worries usually dissolve. That is, until Róisín reminds me about Patient A in Diagram B with the swelling and the nerve damage and lack of mobility.

"I just didn't feel them," I tell her truthfully, explaining my blisters. I walk on tiptoe to avoid excess friction between my heels and my shoes. "I knew they were there all day and I was worried about them before class but then we got dancing and I just forgot."

"One day you're gonna break an ankle and try and dance on it because you 'just forgot'," she sighs.

I smile at my steady feet on the pavement. I tiptoe around a puddle. "Yeah, probably. But honestly it was a lot less blood than it looked like."

Róisín rolls her eyes and we continue our walk home, jabbering here and there about things that had happened in class. Things like who we think will do well at this weekend's feis and who might not, who was checking their phone too often, who has a bad attitude, who didn't show up to class but posted to Instagram, and all other sorts of important things like that.

I live at home, but I have been sleeping in Ro's roommate's bedroom after dance class all summer while her roommate is on an internship. So, that ends up being a good portion of the week. Róisín lives about a mile and a half from the studio and we can drive but whenever we do, Mr. Declan is there to remind us how lazy it is (as well as awful for the sciatic pain both of us have been feeling since we were about fourteen). Sometimes we skateboard, but Mr. Declan would murder us if he ever knew, so we usually stash them behind the bar upstairs from the studio.

And when I say studio, I mean basement. Mr. Declan and his mother rent the cellar space from the Cèilidh Club in town. It's actually fairly nice down there as well, with chairs and a bar for the céilí nights and trad sessions that can't be contained upstairs. Although it has been a common complaint from Declan that it's a shame he can't have a shot every time we forget our steps, it has been the home of the Rooney Academy Dancers for as long as I have known it.

That being said, we have no mirrors but for a few big antique ones that Mr. Declan only lets us take out when he wants us to drill something individually and the floor is tile over concrete. Róisín is convinced that we will have no cartilage left in our knees by thirty if we even have any left now. Most Irish dance studios could probably do with being a little nicer, if only for having some sprung floors, and some surely do, but that tends to go against the spirit of Irish dance. In Irish Dance, we're taught that the best happiness comes from hardship and the sweetest success is sown from sorrow.

It's a badge of honor, to be able to bat our mascaraed lashes with a charming smile after months of blood, sweat, and tears. And that goes for whether you're wearing a sash on the top of the podium or clapping for the girl who is when you've earned the title of dead last.

But I have just one quibble: could we not still say that we worked harder than anyone else did, even if we had sprung floors? Those floors are like dancing on a cloud, for sure, but you'll still sweat just as hard as you would on any other.

I suppose it's going against the Irish aesthetic of the literal and metaphorical perpetual rainy day but still, I have to wonder.

Chapter 2

Not two seconds after we have walked through the door, I drop my dance bag like an 8 AM class and begin my ritual of post-dance-class-whining. "I'm hungry *and* sleepy. The question is do I sleep or do I eat?"

"Why not both?" Róisín asks. She hangs up her team sweatshirt on a hook by the door and shakes her curls out.

I widen my eyes dramatically and unlock my phone. I wave it wildly, showing her the time that reads 9:25. "Because you can't do both at the same time, Ro-shee. Obviously."

"Are you gonna shower?"

The whine that escapes me is that of a six year old. No, not even a six year old. A four year old, at very best; one of the baby four-year-olds, with tight new ghillies that hurt their tiny toes.

I collapse on the floor and put my hands over my eyes. "No, you go. I'm gonna sleep here. I'll let the sweat crust on me and I'll use it as a salt scrub tomorrow morning. Very green-chic."

"Ew." Róisín steps over me delicately and climbs up the stairs.

I hear her rustle about in her room for a minute or two and another minute later I hear the flash of water on tile. I vaguely think that an ice bath would be horribly delightful, but once I collapse for the evening I have a hard time becoming un-collapsed; it's a habit that I picked up during my very hectic college experience.

. When I was in college, I would usually leave the house at 6 am, go to school for five hours, the library for three, and then to dance for however many Mr. Declan felt like that night. I would arrive home exhausted to my toes and my basset hound Wutzer would greet me as if it had been a decade since I had last kissed her velvety nose goodbye at the front gate. Too tired to pet her, I would often just curl up in her dog bed, careless of her slobber stains and dried paw prints, and let her lick the sweat off my arms. Aside from being so drained that the idea of brushing my teeth was painful, never mind taking another step, I liked to curled up with Wutzer because that would be the first time I'd stop thinking all day. If I had taken a shower or gone to my bedroom, I might have started to worry about classwork I had due soon or assignments I could have done better. I might get nervous about having to do a partner lab the next day or start trying to figure out if I had spent more money than I had saved.

However, it's hard to worry about all that when an adorable and droopy hound dog is pawing at your hands and nudging at your ribs, offering you a bowl of hot green beans with butter …

I crack an eye open.

"You're not Wutzer," I say, startled. Róisín is sitting cross-legged next to me on the carpet in PJs, her hair wet. She smells of Pantene and lavender.

"Sorry to disappoint." The corner of her mouth tips into a sleepy smile. She nudges the bowl of green beans closer. "Eat."

I shove a forkful in my mouth at the same time that I say, "I fell asleep."

"You need more protein, chickadee. More energy."

I don't think even my mom has ever commented on my protein intake. Like, ever.

"But green beans!" I say as I plunge my fork into the dish enthusiastically.

I am eating as if this is my last meal on earth. I decide in this moment that my last meal on earth will be green beans. I have already been eating them for a week; I have this habit of buying one food, be it macaroni, bread, cereal, green beans, and eating it for a week. For every meal. Róisín does not exactly approve.

Well, no one really approves.

Tonight she decides to put her moccasined foot down. "Tomorrow, I teach you to make chicken."

"When?" I ask. I struggle into a standing position and make my way from where I collapsed at the bottom of the stairs to the kitchen. I put too much dish soap in my bowl and fill it with hot water. Lazily swishing it around, I say, "Before our morning run, after our 10 o'clock kiddos, or between yoga stretch at five and soft shoe technique at seven?"

Just then Róisín's and my phone both go off in different places of the house (her ringer is "Carrigdance", mine is "Dance of Love". Once a Saoirse, always a Saoirse.)

Her phone sounds like it's coming from the living room and so she scurries across the black and white tile into the next room. I know that mine still has to be in my dance bag where I threw it on the stairs. I do a couple switch-switch-leaps down the hall and find that the force of my throw had actually made my phone fall out of my bag, causing it to bounce inside a muddy black rain boot.

My notifications dash is alight with text messages. Our dance class has a group chat and with 14 girls, it can sometimes be hard to keep up with. I scroll quickly through until I find what seems to be getting everyone in a tizzy.

Cat: Technique at the beach (and yoga) at 5. Be there or be square.

Kasey: Why did we never think of this? ☺ Declan?!

Cat: Just go to the beach, I have my devious ways.

Kat: uhhh

Anya: Kitten is in!

Kat: Anya says I'm bringing pineapple. Apparently.

Quirk: Me and Y are in! And bringing suits! Assuming we should bring sneakers, ya?

Y: I'll bring my dance square thingies!!!

Deidre: omg this is gonna be amazing Declan is gonna drown us

Quirk: even if he doesn't show we should make it the best practice ever and like hashtag it beachtechnique

Rach: HA #RAD

Cat: p.s. I need Róisín and Elodie to aid my devious ways oh Ro and El hello hello Ro and El!!!

After that there were just dozens of girls "shouting" our names and either agreeing to this beach venture or questioning it.

"What is this?" I yell to Róisín.

I'm already scrambling to my feet to meet her in the living room. I fling myself beside her on the old leather couch and snuggle into a corner.

She shrugs then smirks. "Dunno, but I guess I'm not teaching you how to cook."

I pull up the weather on my phone. Tomorrow is supposed to be a balmy 92 degrees. I grin at my friend. "And I guess I won't be buying any tan for this weekend's feis."

Chapter 3

Dance is supposed to teach patience.

When you are five, you learn to wait your turn in line to show off your 123s, your arms flailing everywhere and your toes turned in, just so your teacher might give you a high five.

When you are eight, you learn the phrase "practice makes perfect". And then you learn that for all of your patient practicing, perfect once is not good enough. You need perfect three times. You need better posture, and higher tippy-toes than last time.

When you are eleven, you learn that just because you have waited to hear your number for first, it does not have to come. Even if you've danced the hop jig at five feiseanna in a row. Even if your teacher has overheard a judge saying that you have some of the most impressive hornpipe timing for an intermediate your age. Even still, that doesn't mean you're ever going to get out of dancing that stupid dance, the one you can't do without humming pop-goes-the-weasel (because that's how Miss Orla taught you to hear the difference between hop jigs and regular jigs), with all the other babies.

And God, for all your teen years, you're meant to learn to be patient during your teacher's lectures and when learning difficult steps that just never seem to ever click and when feiseanna run over 2 bazillion hours.

But for all those occasions that I have learned to get through with making a minimum of annoyed, disgusted, and/or bored faces, I am really an awfully impatient person.

I quite literally pop out of bed in the morning.

I throw open the curtains like I am Snow White and though you probably wish I was lying, I call out my open window to a stray cat sitting on our trashcan, "Good morning, trash kitty! And isn't it grand?" Granted, it isn't a loud shout but it is shouted nonetheless.

After greeting trash-cat, I hop about my room, finding my bathing suit, a towel, sunscreen, and anything else I might need at the beach. I decide not to shower because Ro and I are going for a run anyway and, as I wore a pinney and shorts to bed, I find myself suitable enough to take on the neighborhood at 7 AM.

Róisín is watching *Antiques Roadshow*, just as she does every morning that she wakes up before me. Which is, of course, every morning.

Her eyes are glued to the old RCA that sits on top of the chipped blue dresser that Ro's roommate found on the sidewalk. She is tracing the alphabet in thin air with her toes, lazily twisting her ankles. "Phil brought his mother's mirror and combs and things from Italy; his kids made him do it."

I sit down on the floor to tie my sneakers. A little man with slick gray hair is crying. "Worth nothing?"

Róisín shakes her head and untwists her bent limbs to standing. "No, it's worth like 75 thousand. He's gonna donate some of it to the library she used to work at."

I know Róisín is ready without asking and I begin to walk towards the back door. It takes Ro a few seconds to put on her running shoes and then we're off into the not-too-hot-yet June sun.

We jog for a few minutes in companionable silence, our footfalls echoing off the concrete and reaching for the faraway clouds on this quiet morning.

I break the silence at the first corner.

"If I were to ever suddenly come into 75 thousand dollars," I say, already panting. Running is probably my least favorite form of exercise ever. I just feel like I'm never getting anywhere. Dance is flying. Running is. Well … just losing oxygen without any style.

"If you were to ever suddenly come into 75 thousand dollars," Róisín repeats for me. She jumps over a branch with grace. She runs like she dances: beautifully and easily. If she weren't my best friend, I would probably spend a lot of time envying her. To be honest, I spend quite a bit of time doing that even though she is.

"First things first I would pay off my student loans and probably buy my parents some stuff and then move to Ireland. From there I would buy myself a cute little house with a little shed out back for dancing in. I'd teach classes and practice all day every day and maybe go to Irish college if I felt like it, but not like summer-coláiste-whatever like Declan says we all need to go to so we can learn what real suffering is like, real college, and I'd live happily ever after. Amen."

Róisín snorts and crosses herself. "Amen."

I glance at my watch. We haven't even been running five minutes. I need so much more nonsense to discuss. "Oh, oh! And I'd buy out that store you got all those clothes at when you went to All-Irelands, what is it?"

"Penneys!"

"Yes!" I shriek so loudly that an old man, who is eating breakfast on his porch across the street, drops a knife in surprise. "I don't even care about making it to Worlds! Why be a champ when you can look like a champ, with just a portion of the price and zero dance-related suffering?"

"You should be their spokesperson."

I huff a sort of agreeing huff, winded as I am. Since I am currently not-quite-in-college, she knows suggestions like being a spokesperson for a department store across the Atlantic are always appreciated.

The long short of it is this: my parents are used to expecting a lot from me, and I am used to them being used to that.

I was top ten in high school. Varsity lacrosse. I got a community service award or two. I paved a road of perfect report cards and mostly-endeared teachers for my twin sisters, Cora and Evvy (which they have more than fulfilled, to my parents' delight. I mean, who isn't going to be charmed to *tears* by a pair of volleyball playing twins on the mock trial team?)

College offered similar parental pats-on-the-back: I was studying education and history, I had a 4.0, and I literally had my name written (well, carved in a fit of study-boredom-induced-madness but we won't split hairs) on a carrel in the library. Then it just got awful.

I did not have to teach people to love and learn history; I had to stand on a stage and act. My professors did not like the way I talked, the way I dressed, the way I walked (read: danced) in front of the class. I did not pay enough attention to the common cores, my objectives were irrelevant or unclear, my lessons were "unnecessary." I hated it.

It wasn't about telling the stories of the past, investigating and interpreting. It was about ticking boxes off a list of state mandated lessons.

Suddenly my GPA plummeted. Teachers did not adore me. They detested me. I detested them.

For the first time, I hated school. I hated learning.

Then I did the horrible, awful, no good, bad thing and kinda-sorta dropped out.

Now I'm wondering if you've kinda changed the picture in your mind of me to some JD girl, like a punk with ragged hair and thick eyeliner and who flips off cops when they walk by. But honestly, as much as I like to pretend I'm a punk, for all my fantastic black eyeliner and tattoo Pinterest boards, really I'm an innocent little Irish dancer. One who once on a feis trip accidentally stole a stuffed giraffe from a Target, drove five miles away, then drove back, heart pounding, and cried to the manager, "Please don't arrest me! I'm in National Honor Society and I don't think they allow that." One who woke up singing this morning because she was excited to play not-quite-hooky at the beach. I don't know what I am, but I don't think it's a JD.

After lots of crying and lots of "I'm so disappointed in you"s, I handed my parents an outline of my future that I had written sometime after I came tenth to last at Nationals, the year I realized I'd never be Saoirse or any other kind of prima rince-rina. It was a map, if you will, to the Irish dance fountain of youth: the TCRG. Teagascóir Choimisiúin le Rinci Gaelacha.

To become a certified Irish dance teacher.

Though mom and dad were not happy, they said okay. They would support me. I teach classes for Mr. Declan to pay for my lessons and feiseanna.

And so that is the long of it. The short of it is this:

I have a deadline.

Oireachtas.

It is in 2 weeks.

I must qualify for Worlds.

It's terrifying. But for the first time since I was seventeen, seeing Róisín off to Worlds for the third time, I have hope that I can prove to people that I am deserving of Irish dance. Because I love it.

Róisín is my biggest cheerleader in the entire world and always has been. And while she hushes me up anytime I start getting impatient with the future and start assuming failure, she is kind enough to offer me back up plans when she thinks I might need them, as I do on this morning's run. Other suggestions she has offered:

- Open an Etsy shop to sell only the most perfect acorn caps and blades of grass for whistling purposes.
- Somehow take the pageant world by storm- this probably involves whittling?
- McDonalds (plusses include free apple pie).
- Learn set dance tunes on ukulele and become a YouTube sensation.
- Become a blanket thief and thieve the fluffiest blankets from peoples' homes and from stores. Create a shortage and start a fluffy blanket black market.
- Start a heavy shoe black market and/or fight club.
- Enroll in a scientific study. Any study. Except the gross kind.

A block from the house, I am dragging, prancing on my toes because my heels are tired of being dragged down to the pavement.

"Let's sprint." Tears spring to my eyes as I choke out the words.

"*What?*" The sun is beating down hot on us already and Róisín has sweat dripping down her neck.

"Go!" I cry.

We run, steady together and my legs are like rubber bands, whipping out from under me whether I want it or not and I'm actually pulling out in front of Ro to cross over the finish line of our driveway when:

"EL!"

Her long nails scrape at my bicep and my body goes cold with sweat as it hurtles towards the brick driveway. My knee is hot. I am screaming-laughing-shrieking.

"OhmyGodEl! Elodie! Are you alright?" Róisín is frantic.

I am curled up on the driveway, clutching my knee in one hand and a loose brick in another. I don't know if I'm crying because of the pain or because of laughing.

Finally, I unroll a little bit. Blood is streaming from my knee like watercolors, wrapping around my calf and down to my ankle. "Ro-Shee I'm too sweaty!"

"You're *bleeding*, Ellie!" she extends a hand to help me up. Finally, she laughs with me. "Can you drop the freaking brick, already? You need to wash up so we can go teach."

I drop the brick immediately. Like I said, I'm impatient; I know that getting to the Cèilidh Club early won't make us get to the beach any quicker, but I feel like it will. "It's okay! Let's just go like this. I'm gonna tell Dec this is my new feis look. Fierce Elodie Kennedy is taking names and taking blood."

Róisín tries to walk towards the front door but I don't allow it. I aim for the back of her shirt that proclaims "Rooney Academy Dancer" in silver glitter and drag her back towards the street.

I gesture to my knee. "I'm not washing this off till the Oireachtas."

Róisín begins to shove me towards one of the neighbor's sprinklers; I scream. If the block wasn't awake yet, they are now.

Chapter 4

The rules to 123s of Death are simple: don't die.

"Don't let me kill you," I warn.

Of course, this causes the pack of black-clad seven year olds before me to giggle. I shunt them into a circle in the middle of the floor.

"Why is your knee all bloody?" one of the cutest, littlest, freckliest-faced boys in the world asks me.

I slide his socked (shoe-less) foot into fifth position.

"Because I wasn't wearing shoes!" I chide him. "I slipped during 123s of death and slid *all* the way across the floor."

His brother is on the other side of the circle. He squints at me. "There's not a bloody spots!"

I squint back. "Or maybe there's so much blood there are no spots, eh?"

Ten tiny shocked faces turn their mouths to thoughtful Os, making me laugh.

"So! Ways to not die," I say. I begin walking around the circle, tucking in loose shoelaces and rolling back shoulders. "Tippy toes, straight arms, thumbs in, turn-out, butt kicking, hoppity hops …"

I tick off more things than I truly believe a second grader can manage to think about at one time but that I hope they might one day learn to.

"Timing!" I am back at the stereo. "But what's most important?" I ask.

"Don't let you kill us!" one girl shouts.

"Smile!" I correct, offering my own.

She covers her mouth and giggles back. "Oh!"

I hit play and wink. "But don't let me kill you either."

It's same feis record that I have been listening to since I, too, was seven. The music swells over the speakers and I count my kiddos off ("five, six, and off you go!") and they start dancing.

123s of Death is an elimination game. Any bad technique, I call out the bad form and the kid and start two piles, a "maybe" and an "out". The music goes until there is one kid left. They win the first round, but then "maybe" pile gets another chance to dance against the winner. It's kind of like a recall and is a good little mental prep for competitions. They get used to me not caring who wins or loses; everyone gets a high five. They sweat and compete and, it seems, have fun.

They seem particularly pleased today when Róisín comes skipping down the stairs, still covered in glitter from her pre-school fairy party. The kids are all trying to get her attention without waving, which would compromise their posture, when she goes Benedict Arnold on them and hops into their circle.

They stop trying to catch the eye of their BFF Miss Róisín, the champ, and pout at me.

"No fair!"

"Miss Elodie!"

"She's gonna win!"

And for a moment, I toy with them. I twirl my non-existent mustache and I let out some loud, thoughtful "hmm"'s. But the looks of disappointment, the little frowns and crinkled foreheads, worrying that maybe not a single one of them would win because this *towering* 5-foot-4, big-girl-princess just came waltzing in like she owned their class …

Well, I simply couldn't crush my wee babs like that.

"Out!" I cry. "She's got floppy toes, wiggly arms, and her heels are on the ground. Frankly, I don't know why you thought you ever could dance among legends like Molly Mumford, Prince Danny, or Miss Maeve-y! Any of them, really."

Róisín hops out of their circle. "But I love the dance!" she twirls across the floor, careening into me. We both crash into Declan's director chair.

"Ahh, well we'll have to keep you then," I say, teasingly poking her in the arm. "Anyone who loves the dance is always welcome here."

The kids have taken this silly display as an opportunity to stop dancing and have thrown their sweaty selves onto the tile in fits of mad laughter. They have forgiven Róisín, not to mention that they're probably delirious with the heat. Despite having four fans going and being underground, the wet, hot air from the parking lot seeps through the street level windows and has made our brains soggy.

"So what is Cat's grand plan?" I ask Ro. I keep one eye on the kids, who are rolling around on the ground, as senseless as earthworms.

"Oh," Róisín laughs, a grin immediately tugging at the corners of her mouth. "It's great. So Cat's dad is taking Mr. Declan out to lunch in the city and then she's supposed to drive him back here for class. Poor Kitty has only had her license for a month though, so she might just take the wrong exit."

I glance at the kiddos, who are currently having a dust bunny fight. People trust me with these children. Can you believe it?

"Hey! Creeps," I shout over their high-pitched tones. "Go get drinks and change into hard shoes, yeah? Little sips of water!"

The pack of tiny dancers (gaggle? rafter? murder? If you had spent as much time with these precious angels as I have, you would probably go with murder) skip and stumble to their pile of bags and I turn back to Róisín.

"So what's our part in these shenanigans?" I ask.

"Well," she says. "Actually pretty simple. All we have to do is lock the doors and tell them upstairs that we're having class elsewhere."

I think of the darling, gruff barman upstairs. His name is Thomas, he is about seventy, and he has the slightest hint of a brogue beneath his white mustache. Sometimes he can be so adorably stern and worried when he thinks we girls are running ourselves ragged with too much dancing, bringing us pitchers of icy water and trays of cookies, tutting and berating Mr. Declan as he pinches the little ones on the cheeks and giving us hugs of strength.

But mostly I am thinking of the times he has come barreling down the stairs at a full .25 miles an hour, shaking his fist and shouting incoherently because unsupervised sessions have gotten too loud and all of a sudden someone is clinging to the rafters and there are broken jars of maraschino cherries spilling their red guts like blood everywhere . . .

Yeah, times, plural...

"Thomas is working?" I mentally cross my fingers for the negatory.

Ro nods and reaches down to her dance bag. She comes out clutching a Ziploc baggie of crumbling, mix-matched biscuits. "If you're hungry ..."

I shrug and grab a chocolate covered digestive. After all, it isn't every day we get to eat them stateside.

"Okay so we don't tell Thomas. We leave him a note! Don't ask permission, ask forgiveness." As the first-born child of very strict parents, I am extremely skilled in this art.

"Miss Elodie, Cara isn't putting on her shoes and you told us to put on our hard shoes and I want to practice the St. Patrick's Day for the feis this weekend--" Cara's cousin Tessie talks at a high-pitched mile per minute. She is still tattling about Cara not putting on her shoes and asking questions about her costume when I gently tap a finger on her mouth.

"No!" I say, firmly. I feel her pulling a pout. "I will talk to your cousin. Okay?"

She nods and I take my hand away. I wipe seven-year-old slime on my shorts and prop her up on her coltish legs.

"Go on and practice and I'll watch you in a minute." I turn around. "Now as for you Miss Cara, why *aren't* those shoes on? Does Miss Róisín have to start the clock?"

Cara sticks her tongue out at me because I am already halfway through tying her right shoe for her; she knows that even if I did time her for a shoe change, I would help her through it.

The thing is, she is really a cute kid and I would hate to see her cry or something. I've made two kids cry already this year. Once I didn't feel too bad, because the girl wasn't listening to me at all and I had probably told her ten times already in class to kick her bum during threes. She kept giving me blank stares half the time and the other half she was too busy talking with her friends to hear me. Finally I told her that if she wasn't going to dance she would have to sit out because she was just distracting me from the other girls and that's when she started the waterworks.

She hid in the corner for ten minutes and then it took another five for me to convince her that *I do* want her to dance, I just want her to kick her bum when she does it, as well.

Okay, so I felt a little bad.

The other time I just felt plain awful.

I accidentally kneed a little girl in the mouth. She didn't bleed or anything, it just happened that she was so bitty that when my knee came up, her face happened to be in the strike zone. They tell you Irish dance isn't a contact sport, so just imagine me trying to explain to a concerned mother why her little sobbing angel had a fat lip.

Sometimes I wonder why Mr. Declan trusts me with these kids, particularly when one combines my childcare prowess with my ongoing struggle to be a decent dancer, but it's what I've got.

And that should probably prevent me from doing what Róisín and I are about to do.

Róisín flips over a cardboard coaster and writes in impossibly tiny script. "Okay, sign your name under, 'you can find us on the web at #RooneySeasideSwag.'"

I sign my name in full and sprinkle some endearing (smartass) hearts around it.

It should probably stop me...

... But of course, it doesn't.

Chapter 5

It's a well-known fact that when a dancer is at the beach, a dancer *must* take artsy dance pictures.

What it is about leap pictures on the beach, I couldn't tell you, but it's like this strange collective compulsion. Maybe it's because all of us have spent our childhoods being jealous of our ballerina friends and their dance poster-pasted walls, which always seemed to include some stock images of a black and white arabesque on the seaside. I'd ask where they found so many posters and they would shrug disinterestedly, kicking a soccer ball against the wall or flipping the pages of a yearbook, and reply vaguely, "I dunno, the store."

Ah, the luxury of being a tutu-wearer.

That all being said, my teammates are taking full advantage of our clandestine class location. Via social media, I've seen that trio leap photos are quite literally abounding and our school name is etched in the sand.

"Let's go, let's go!" I squeal the second Róisín parks the jeep in the nearly empty lot. I can see a small pile of dance bags under a pavilion. I can hear the other girls laughing and shouting and I can't wait to get down there with them. I have not been to the beach all summer and I know some of the others haven't had the chance either. The Cèilidh Club is like my second home (or third, if you count Ro's house) but every now and again I find myself dragging to class, the prospect of a sweaty basement that always smells faintly of corned beef and cabbage suddenly just a little depressing to me.

So when I kick off my shoes and race down the sun-warmed sand, I feel like the salty air is clearing the corned beef out of my lungs and I just know that I'm going to dance well tonight.

"Well, what's the craic?" a deep voice hushes our girlish din of excitement.

That is if our TC doesn't kill us first.

Jax falls out of her leap mid-air, Rach and Y fall out of handstands, and incriminating phones are thrown into the sand, all while a stunned Róisín nearly is pulled out by the tide.

We all take in the scene before us: Mr. Declan is looking displeased, to say the least, and Cat is tripping behind him while yelping pleas of, "Have a heart, Dec!"

In the next moment, there is a scramble for traction on the sand and we spend a few moments bumping into each other trying to make a straight-ish line, torn between laughter and tears. We peer at each other's feet as if we don't remember what fifth position feels like without a mirror to show us.

When we have finally figured it out, we look to Mr. Declan. The pride we felt over tricking our TC is slowly turned to fear as Mr. Declan stares at us, not saying a word. I force a grimace on my face, hoping that I don't look too reprehensible.

"Are ye serious?" Mr. Declan throws his hands in the air and attempts to make eye contact with each of us. When he gets to me, I kind of shrug one shoulder like, *I guess, I mean we are at the beach, yeah?*

"It's good advertisement?" Cat says, peeking around Mr. Declan's back, which is where she has been hiding. She plucks at the edge of her shorts. offering a feeble look of adoration to Mr. Declan. "So everyone can see what a team oriented art Irish dance is, with good-humored, merciful teachers and …"

She wilts under his glare and hurries to join our haphazard line. Mr. Declan tracks her path and then he does something horrifying-- he smiles. You know that scene in *The Grinch Who Stole Christmas* when the Grinch grins and his eyes go all narrow and his hair curls from the potent evil of his plans?

Well, Mr. Declan is a dead ringer.

"Ahh, Cat," Declan says. He strolls over to our friend and claps a hand on her shoulder. He pretends that he is taller than she is and crouches a bit. "You've a ten minute reel, don't you?"

Cat wants to die; we all know, because we suddenly want to kill her for this plan.

But no one says a word, because we agreed and besides, we are weeks away from the Oireachtas. Call us crazy, but not too deep down we know a ten minute reel is what we need.

Cat hands Mr. Declan her phone and smiles. "Actually, it's eleven and a half!"

Mr. Declan has us move down to the packed, wet sand on the shoreline and, music in hand, off we go. For twelve minutes, I forget my parents' ultimatum and my worries that I won't place high enough at the Oireachtas or that I've made an awful mistake dropping out and that I'm going to make an awful dance teacher or, God forbid, about my protein intake. For eleven and half precious minutes I feel free, then like I can't breathe, and when I work through that, I am in a cloud of bliss; I feel my aching lungs, cool breezes, and legs strong enough to carry me across oceans.

For eleven and a half minutes, I am hardly human. For eleven and half minutes, I am a dancer (Man, I can really identify with that Killers song).

I barely notice the music stop over my heaving breath. Mr. Declan tells us to walk it out and I follow the other girls in a haze of endorphins, ready for my next hit.

Mr. Declan lets us break for a quick stretch and some water but then hits us hard. We do ladders of all our soft shoe dances, stacking from one step to five steps and back down again, and while we wait for our next turn, he has us alternation between core and arms. It isn't easy, even on the packed sand.

Next, we are doing the same with our sneakers on the movable tiles Y brought, but alternating with drills. My energy has hardly waned when suddenly I notice the sun has disappeared from sight and that the light has slowly dripped away. I nudge Róisín. "How long have we been here?"

She tilts her head like a befuddled puppy, looking unsure of whether we have been here for hours or days.

"Girls, if you've brought your towels bring 'em here so we can stretch," Mr. Declan instructs.

We arrange ourselves in a semi-circle facing the ocean. Despite the towel I have laid down, I already have sand clinging to every sweaty inch of my body. But I could care less. As I roll myself out into a straddle and reach my fingers out as far in front of me as they can go, I think to myself that the feeling of being so spent is maybe better than anything in the world. A well-earned stretch is more delicious than chocolate and I would trade half the chocolate in the world just to feel this accomplished at the end of every day. This trade would be good for me, as my idea of eggs for breakfast usually involves the Cadbury variety.

"Now girls, I ain't mad at ya …" and so goes the typical start of a Mr. Declan speech. Tonight's speech goes:

"Now girls, I ain't mad at ya for wanting to have a bit of fun. You've been training hard this summer, working hard for all your competitions. I'm mad at ya for kidnapping me." He glares at Cat and we can't help but laugh. Then he turns on Ro and I. "And I'm disappointed in ye for not discouraging it."

Ah, that disappointed tone. I feel my face flush all the way to the roots of my hair but I can't help the giggle that escapes. I try to smother my laughter in my knees.

"You're laughing and I'm very serious here!" Mr. Declan says, laughing oh so ironically.

I sit up straight and cry through my laughter, "I'm sorry! I'm sorry!" Then I take a deep breath and smile sincerely. "Really, though."

He pinches his fingers so there is an inch of space between them, asking me if that is how sorry I am. I mimic the motion and nod, laughing a little more.

Mr. Declan shakes his head. "That's what I thought. Flex."

I let my hands relax on my thighs as I stretch my toes up off the sand towards the dusky sky.

Mr. Declan strolls along the beach. "I just wanted to tell you girls how proud I am of you tonight though, really. You really deserve to give yourselves a pat on the back because I don't know when I've ever seen all of ye working so hard at once."

For a few long moments, there is a choked hush, of waves lapping at the shore as the tide goes out farther and farther. Our brains try to work out the gravity of Mr. Declan saying he was proud of us for what had begun as a juvenile, elaborate plan for an easy class.

"Thank-you," Róisín says at last.

The other girls are shaken out of their shock and begin to mutter and mumble the same. I look up from my stretch at Mr. Declan, my eyes hopeful.

"You, too," he smiles.

I feel my cheeks go red again as I murmur my thanks.

My heart drums and I feel the tremble of a spark. *You could place at the Oireachtas,* it whispers.

It isn't the dream I have been having for months: the one where Mr. Declan takes me aside and says that he knows I have it in me. Of him whooping when I recall and rushing to hug me onstage when I place.

It isn't the dream, but it's close enough. I am imagining my crying face (waterproof make-up, so no raccoon eyes) and the photos that would follow, when suddenly I find myself torn out of my daydream as I realize that there are hands clamped around my wrists and ankles.

"Wh-uh?!" It appears that the girls had noticed the depth of my reverie and had used the moment to engage in an ambush. I am lifted into the air as Mr. Declan, the big so-and-so, shouts, "And our first ice bath volunteer of the evening is our own Elodie Kennedy!"

I am shrieking and kicking up sand but despite my current training schedule, I'm no match for thirteen other girls; I blame my utter dedication to dreams and my low protein intake.

Before I can say "I hate you" three times and summon the King of the Fairies, a co-conspirator of Mr. Declan's who is fond of stamina drills (or so was our interpretation of the legend), I find myself tasting salt on my tongue as I clench my eyes tight against the freezy foam. My body rolls, tangled in seaweed, as I'm tugged out by the tide.

I come up gasping and ready to fight them all. I'm shrieking all sorts of menacing threats at my lovely teammates. They surround me, up to their knees in the sea. I toss myself sideways like a fish on deck, hoping to take them all out swiftly with enough flailing.

"No!" Róisín is doubled over with laughter as well as the weight of Rachel clinging to her back like a bedraggled urchin.

"Let's get Declan," she tries to convince me, splashing water at my face. I wrestle with her and Kate until I have dunked them both to my satisfaction. They come up sputtering, looking like drowned rats.

Pleased with my work, I shrug primly. "Mr. Declan is waiting, ladies."

Fourteen teenaged girls struggling to run in water must look like some sort of comical zombie scene to Mr. Declan and that would explain why he is laughing. That is, until he finds hands shoving at his back and pulling at his arms.

"Now girls!" he tries to be stern but we are driven. The tracksuit needs the saltwater treatment. "No no no no no!"

"You need more protein, Mr. Declan!" I shout over my shoulder, my hands gripping one of his flailing ankles.

He is no match for fourteen major-ready girls either. I figure he must be proud. After all, he is the one who trained us.

After offering Declan to the icy sea, we are all too tired to do much more than sit at the edge of the water and let the tides rush around us. We all kind of lament the lack of sun but I can't help but feel entirely content.

For a while, I listen to Kate natter on about how excited she is for her boyfriend to come to the feis this weekend. This is more exciting than the first time he came; we all agree that for anyone to return to a feis after experiencing it as a mere spectator ... well, he must really like Kate.

"Do you want to win for him?" I ask thoughtfully, my chin resting on my knees.

She swishes the water around with her hands. "I mean, it'd be nice but I know I don't have to. Last time, I wanted to. Like, I trained so hard, taking privates every weekend and practicing even when I got home from class. I wanted to be just so perfect for him. But while I was dancing I just saw Jack in the audience and … I don't know." Kate shrugs and smiles. "I just realized he didn't need me to be perfect, being with me in my element, or whatever, was enough."

I almost feel tears sting at my eyes, the thought is so nice.

"Aww," the girls coo over Kate's sappiness.

She splashes us all and grins. "Shut up! Besides, last time he came he bought me Starbucks and Thai food, as a reward, so I'd like to repeat that."

"So who are you trying to be perfect for, Elodie?" Róisín wiggles her eyebrows. Ugh, her and her knowing my entire life and practice schedule.

I laugh. "Oh ya know, my Irish boyfriend. The famous bodhrán player. He saw me dancing and fell in love with the fact that although dance hates me, still I persevere!"

"I've figured it out," Róisín says, a definite tone to her voice. "You're trying to be perfect for dance. Dance doesn't hate you. Dance doesn't ask you to do anything; you just want to be perfect because you love it. You're in love, Ellie!"

"Should I change my relationship status on Facebook?" I ask, burying my feet in the sand. "Dance hasn't bought me any green curry yet."

She nods furiously. "Oh yeah. You're in deep. Committed. No one is coming between you two."

I glance down at my sandy toes and smile.

I can't help it; you're always grinning about stupid things when you're in love.

Chapter 6

Two days after the Great TC Kidnapping of 2k16, we all have our last feis before the Oireachtas. This requires waking up at 5 AM to shower, doing our make-up, and curling my hair so we can reach the venue (2 hours away and the next state over) by 10 so we can watch all our wee babs dance.

I am excited and nervous, like I am always on feis day, but also a little glum. I am glum because I have to wear my old school dress rather than the new solo dress, which has been made just for me. Seeing as I couldn't afford a new dress, I was overjoyed when a studio mom offered to make me one in exchange for private lessons for her little boys. It was a fantastic trade-off, as her kids are two of the cutest cuties that have ever Irish danced. And not only that, but it was a welcome change from the petite prima donnas that normally jigged about the Cèilidh Club.

But most of all it was fantastic because my dress is gorgeous. It's a black velvet three panel with a high collar edged with lace. There is very little embroidery, just some trimming around the skirt and sleeves of pale blue, white, and gold knot work, but it has lovely crystals on the bodice.

The thing is Mrs. Casey had to take in some measurements after my final fitting, so that leaves me stuffed into my old school dress. There's nothing wrong with it; really, it's not awfully out of fashion, just plain red with a white satin skirt. But it's small on me and I have been wearing it in its various reincarnations since I was ten.

Not to mention all the other girls from class look like jewels from a treasure chest, all shiny and bright. They are a pile of crystals and sequins, satin and velvet, no color or shade unrepresented. I know it probably looks crazy to the hotel staff but I wonder if any of them recognize the beauty of a solo dress. The way each one is unique, the careful stitching, the stories told in the seams. The best ones are perfectly suited to a dancer, whether they might be lovely or fierce, more traditional or innovative, and accentuate all their wonderful qualities. I don't know if any other sport does quite that.

Aside from my marveling about the uniqueness of Irish dance, the feis is pretty run of the mill. The babies are adorable. The vendors are sparkly. Things run behind schedule. Same old same old until after I finish my heavy round. I forget my half step for hornpipe (Mr. Declan just changed it in class this week for, like, the hundredth time) and fumble around onstage, grimacing at the judges. After I bow, I practically race offstage.

"Great job." I smile at the girl I danced with as I attempt to mop up some of the sweat pouring from my face with the inside of my sleeve.

"You too," she says. "Want me to unzip you?"

"Oh thanks, yes please!" I turn around so she can free me from my prison and then do the same for her.

"I just don't get why these things have to go all the way up to our necks!" she bemoans. "Is this 1862 or something?"

I laugh as I shimmy out of the top part of my dress. "Much better!" I smile at the girl and give her a little goodbye wave. "See you at awards!"

I am standing in the hallway outside the ballroom when one of my wee ones ambushes me. Her name is Zoe: she is four years old, redheaded, and tiny.

"Miss Elodie!" she shrieks as she attaches herself to my leg. "Look at my medal!"

She throws one arm out, showing me a little engraved medal. I reach down to grab it.

I read the back and learn that she has earned 3rd place for her light jig. "Oh wow, congrats! You know, I loved the way you smiled onstage, you looked so confident! I'm so proud."

"Thanks," she chirps, holding out her hand for her prize. When I return it she says, "Are you gonna win a sash Miss Elodie?"

"Hmm," I say thoughtfully. "Walk with me."

With Zoe still firmly attached, I begin stumping my way through the clumps of dancers back to the ballroom where I had left my belongings. In the chilly air-conditioned room the sweat on my stomach turns cold, making goosebumps rise up. I rustle through the jumble of spare poodle socks and half-empty cans of hairspray, searching for my track jacket.

I tickle Zoe to detach her from my leg. She collapses to the floor, giggling. I slip on my jacket and sit beside her. "Do *you* think I'll get a sash, Zwee?"

She clambers into my lap. "Well, I think you were the best, so probably. I think you'll probably get one!" She beams up at me.

"Aw shucks." I play at being bashful, scrunching up my nose and sticking out my tongue at her. "Nah, you're the best!"

"No you!"

I tickle her in the ribs again and she falls all over the place laughing. We are still going back and forth about who is the best when Róisín appears, grinning.

"I vote Zwee, 'cause she and I are besties. Right, Zwee?" she says. Zoe nods furiously.

I look up at her, still laughing. "Rude!"

Róisín has an armful of medals. "Help me with awards?" she asks.

"Sure!" I give Zoe a quick hug and leap to my feet. Róisín and I walk to the second ballroom where primary awards had been scheduled to start an hour and a half ago.

"Thanks," Ro says. "It was supposed to be Sarah Murphy and that Colm Kelly from Inish Rince, or whatever, but last anyone saw they said they were going to Starbucks. Take third and fourth?"

I have just arranged the medals on my arms when the TC from Inish Rince, Cora, appears beside us. She is the one running this feis.

"Hi!" I greet her. Instead of replying, she frowns.

"What's your name?" she asks.

"Elodie Kennedy," I explain brightly. "It was supposed to be Colm and Sarah but I don't mind helping."

"Oh …" she glances me up and down. Slowly I feel the smile slipping off my face. I was not expecting applause for helping out or anything, but I wasn't expecting *this* either.

At last, she says, "I can't let you go to awards looking like that. Just … no."

I look down at my team jacket and my short, tight spandex shorts and then at Róisín, in her perfectly prim navy romper with the scalloped edges.

"Oh," I echo Cora, a catch in my throat. "Okay. Okay then …"

Slowly I hand Róisín the medals. She is staring at Cora, puzzled.

"Sorry," Ro whispers.

I shake my head, feeling tears biting at my eyes.

When I am out of the ballroom, my eyes begin to blur. Sniffling, I rush to the bathroom, hoping I can save my eyeliner.

It is crowded at the mirrors. I take a tissue and dab delicately at my eyes. My cheeks are red with embarrassment.

"Are you alright, honey?" a concerned mom asks me.

I nod and attempt a smile. "Oh yeah! I just have this thing. It's just allergies," for unknown reasons I continue to ramble. "And I was re-watching Gossip Girl last night and like God, why do Chuck and Blair have to do this thing? Just be together, already, you're both crazy. And the whole ring plot? Like, ugh, emotions all over the place. But yeah, I'm fine! No worries."

She rubs my back, frowning, and then walks away.

Ten minutes later, my eyes have finally stopped tearing and I feel okay to go back to the ballroom. Almost immediately, Lily and Kate rush me.

"We heard," Kate says.

"Yeah, ridiculous! You know she came over to me side stage when I was changing my shoes and I had my dress unzipped just now. She said, 'You Rooney girls should remember that you're setting an example for the younger ones.'"

I think of my conversation with little Zoe. "We're not bad examples!" I then think of the Great TC Kidnapping of 2k16. "Well, not usually. Not today!"

"How can we get back at her?" Kate says.

We throw around ideas like coming to the next feis in bikinis (not immediate enough) and wearing just our sports bras and shorts to accept award (likely disqualification) until we come to a solution: passive aggressiveness via Instagram. Imagining her reaction is all the satisfaction we need.

We gather up the other girls from class and they listen to the story indignantly, their mouths open.

"So we're gonna take a picture of us in just our jackets and spandex and post it on the 'gram," Lily says excitedly.

Yes, yes. We Irish dancers are of a bad sort.

We pose ourselves grinning in front of the feis banner, taking a variety of prim poses, pretending to hold tea cups and whatnot.

"Caption it 'Having a classy time at the Inish Rince Feis'," Clare says excitedly. Everyone is frantically typing and hashtagging.

We are proud of our juvenile delinquency, as usual. I have honestly nearly forgotten all about Cora the Fashion Police until Mr. Declan strides over to me after awards. I give Róisín a tap to let her know that I'm leaving. I have gotten second to last and I expect him to say something about being disappointed. Instead, he throws an arm around me and says, "You always smile, no matter what place you get. Don't let anyone ever tell you you're a bad influence on the younger ones. I know you're one of the best."

Suddenly I feel silly about the whole Instagram photo. What do I care about what Cora thinks?

I am about to apologize when Mr. Declan says, "you know, you tagged the feis wrong. You put I-N-I-S-S. Show some respect, Elodie."

He winks before strolling off to congratulate the other girls.

Róisín walks over to me, curious. I tell her what Mr. Declan said and she replies, "Yeah, we're lucky to have him. I'll take the Don Dorcha hopeful over the two time world champ any day."

I remind myself to write that on this year's class Christmas card.

Chapter 7

The next two weeks are exhausting. I finally realize Ro might be right about this protein thing.

"I didn't mean to carry around a jar of peanut butter with you!" she cries one night as I whip the jar out during a practice break.

"So that means you don't want any of this celery?" I say.

She frowns and crab-crawls wearily across the floor. "Well, no, I didn't say that."

So in 14 days we turn into peanut butter eating machines whilst making sure our steps are as solid as they are going to get. I'm still nervous because it seems that my steps will never look as great as Róisín's; I won't be as high on my toes, as turned out, as rhythmic. But, nonetheless, I'm feeling pretty confident.

And excited. Really excited.

A major is like … the Kentucky Derby of Irish dance. There are beautiful venues. We all plan our outfits weeks (okay, like, months) in advance. The podium positions are sought after. It's a dream.

And this year the Oireachtas is in Canada and that means passports!

At 1 AM the evening before we leave, I am still laying in my bed staring at the Joe Bitter poster on my ceiling, the one that has Ryan Gosling's face plastered over his (don't ask), when I imagine getting onstage, for the billionth time. I feel my heart rate go through the roof for the billionth time as well.

I text Róisín frantically.

Elodie: I MIGHT BE HAVING A HEART ATTACK?! I FEEL LIKE I'M HAVING A HEART ATTACK. I'M SO NERVOUS/EXCITED I CAN'T RO. IT'S LIKE RODNEY'S GLORY @ 11256 ON MY CHEST.

Ro: It's good cardio :P go to sleeeeeep we have to wake up in five hours!

I toss my phone into a heap of clothes that are on the floor and bury myself deeper under the covers, ignoring the thermostat by the door that is reading 84 F.

"Five hours till we leave," I whisper to myself. Then I grin and kick all the covers off again in excitement.

"Five hours until an adventure!" I shout.

Róisín bangs on the wall between our rooms. "GO TO SLEEP!"

I wake up the next morning to Ro quietly knocking on my door. She is chirping, "Oh Elodie, up and at 'em, Champ."

It's the champ comment that opens my eyes because Rosin isn't teasing at all. I grin and disentangle myself from my sheets. In two seconds flat I launch myself out of bed and yank open the door.

"Road trip to the cottage!" I cry, shoving a fist in the air.

"Road trip to the cottage!" she returns, doing a silly little twirl.

Our first major, our first céilí, our never ceasing battle cry of adventure. Irish dancers: we might not have stock image posters, but we have puns to get us through.

We stumble about the house, half awake and shouting snatches of the Canadian national anthem to each other through the halls as we pack our stuff into the jeep. I take a chilly shower that wakes me up in a more efficient fashion; pull on some yoga shorts and a tank top that says, "Muscles & Mascara."

I am braiding my hair when I cross paths with Ro on her way to the bathroom.

"Can you bring these out?" she says, referencing the dress bags in her hand. I open my mouth, indicating I will carry the five pound apiece dresses with my teeth.

She is unamused. "I'll just leave them here on the floor."

I finish braiding my hair and skip outside where the sun is still gentle in the early hours. I packed my things the night before at home. Mom and dad wanted to have a goodbye/good luck dinner for me, so we had done that, and then I had slept over Ro's so we could leave straight from her house.

I hop into the passenger seat and turn on the radio.

Twenty minutes later, I am still sitting in the passenger seat, sunglasses on, listening to The Wombats crackling through the speakers.

"I thought you were never gonna be ready in time!" Ro jokes as she hops in and turns the ignition. I give her a look and laugh at her, "Ha ha", which makes us laugh for real.

"Road trip to the cottage!" she cries gleefully as we back out of the driveway and away from America.

Since I started dancing, I have never been to a feis without Róisín, or a major. However, the tradition of camping didn't begin until Oireachtas the year that I was 11 and Ro was 12. Our hotel rooms, along with a bunch of other families', had been given away by mistake. Being an unseasonably warm November in New Hampshire, our fathers decided to "gruff" up Irish dance (that statement did not sit well with us, and we spent the weekend challenging them to push-up contests) and they suggested that we stay in some nearby cabins. Thus began the tradition.

Sometimes the other girls joined in, and other times we made late nights of running around the hotels with them until our parents dragged us away, but it was always our thing.

This year we are making the drive on our own for the first time: we can drink as much coffee as we want, pick the music (trashy chart hits and set tunes), and can screech and swear at Siri while on the George Washington to our hearts' content. It really is happiness.

And when we get to the campground in Toronto nearly ten hours later, we are experiencing a different kind of happiness: slap-happiness. We have consumed 100% sugar and 100% caffeine and 0% actual food during our journey. We slept few hours last night. And it shows.

The front desk of the campground is manned by a disinterested looking dude of an undesirable age with an unappealing soul patch. He frowns at us as we block his view of the television that hangs above the door, which appears to be playing a grainy rerun of *Party of Five*, if I am not mistaken. He asks for our names at the same time he turns up the volume.

Ro steps forward with her printed out booking confirmation.

"Róisín O'Shee." She immediately starts giggling, losing it in a way only feis-days Róisín does. "O'Seen. O'--"

I slap a hand down on the counter and cut her off. "No, no, *I'm* the one who rhymes. Elodie Kennedy. I mean to say, I'm Elodie Kennedy, she's Róisín O'Shneen."

Ro and I start laughing all over again and I think Mr. Front Desk Man's soul patch starts to grow before our very eyes, as soul patches grow not from sweet emotions but from emotions of true, deep-seated tumult. Róisín's name has somehow evolved into Rodney So-Clean when the dude just grabs the booking confirmation off of the counter.

"Roy-sin O'Shea," he says. "Just give me the credit card."

"He messed up my name," Róisín whispers not-quietly-at-all as he turns around to bill us.

"And you made me miss this entire episode of *Party of Five*," he shoots back.

"You know it gets cancelled," I say. "Like, twice. Like twenty years ago. You're a bit behind the curve."

His soul patch is now about two feet long with sadness and anger. He shoves Róisín's receipt across the counter. "Oh great. Thanks. And I thought you two loudmouths were the worst thing to happen to me today."

We mime zipping our lips and tiptoe away dramatically. Some people just don't know a good time.

Though, admittedly, *Party of Five* was a fantastic television show.

I can do a passing copy of the Stolen Kiss choreography and bring a old folks home to tears. Róisín can literally do a 16 bar treble reel en pointe.

But good God in heaven, we can't put up a tent.

As mentioned, we normally have parents around or a cabin or, at the very least, other girls to help us flip the directions around a few times until we run out of pieces to stick into other pieces.

We are still shrieking an hour later when Mr. Soul-Patch comes by. His beard has appeared to grow longer, mournfully encouraged by our glee, and I think it will be down to his knees by the time we are gone.

"You're too loud." His monotone suggests that aside from the disappointment we have garnered, he has also reached the second cancellation of *Party of Five*. Tough day.

"Sorry," I say, while trying to stifle a giggle. "It's just that the tent keeps collapsing--"

"Attacking!" Róisín interjects, giving our crumpled aperture the side eye.

I nod. "Yeah. So we are trying but--"

"Quiet hours start now and your voices carry. This is your last warning."

Róisín puts her hands on her hips. I wrinkle my nose. In unison, we say, "Or what, you'll kick us out?"

He raps an entirely unimportant looking badge that has been pinned to an old Hanes t-shirt. "I'm the park ranger so yeah."

Róisín opens her mouth. "Excuse me but--"

"Shh," he hisses. Then he turns on heel and walks away.

"I thought they were meant to have manners in Canada!" I huff.

"He is an insult to his nation." Ro nods.

We turn away from the spot where Mr. Soul-Patch had been and frown at our tent.

"We need to finish this," Ro says.

"We never will," I moan. Just then, my stomach growls; this makes me change my tune very quickly. "Never mind, we gotta. I'm starved. We are cute, clever, and capable. Let's get it done."

So after an hour of falling over laughing and lots of failure, the motivation of food has us finished in fifteen minutes. Typical.

We throw the car into drive moments after pounding the last tent stake into the ground and race off to the nearest eatery. In full feis mode, our mouths take us to the first and greasiest looking diner we see.

It is, of course, perfect.

Despite my stomach being in one continuous rumble, like a roll of thunder, I can't help but bounce around in the typical, torn, red leatherette seats of the booth and fiddle around with the clacky page-turners of the jukebox. As I always do I say, "I wonder if this is a real one or if it just takes your nickel and plays Frankie Valli on a loop?"

"Well, this is Canada so we actually take just your nickel and play Robin Sparkles all day long, regardless," a guy replies.

Jittery with exhaustion and hunger, I bounce around the booth in confusion, looking for the source of the male voice. After what is probably a full minute of my flailing, I look up at a shaggy-haired waiter. He smiles toothily and I feel myself think, *"Now this is the Canadian I've been waiting for!"*

What I say is, "How did you know we're American?"

He replies very seriously, "You look American. Your footsteps fall in time with 'America the Beautiful' and your perfume reeks of freedom."

Róisín and I laugh, prompting the cute Canadian to do the same.

"Actually," he admits. "It was your saying, 'wow, Canadian diners look just like American diners!'"

I feel myself blush and Róisín sticks out her tongue in a way that communicates what she's thinking: *"Typical El. Typical."*

"What were you expecting?" He asks curiously.

I shrug. "More moose, less muscle cars. And maybe more maple syrup." I give him a concerned look. "Speaking of ... could I get a vehicle for some maple syrup? A stack of chocolate chip pancakes, perhaps?"

He clicks a pen and begins jotting down my order. "I couldn't dream of letting you down again."

"Good man."

"And you, my more reasonable American friend?" He winks at Ro and takes her order.

In no time, Ro and I are gorging ourselves on pancakes, eggs, and the most delicious maple syrup this side of Vermont. We decide the syrup is actually ambrosia and put some in a takeaway ketchup container to taste between rounds tomorrow.

As we are paying our check, our friendly waiter gives us a bit of local advice. "Hey, just so you guys know, right up the road there's a drive-in that does double features. It's only ten a carload if you're looking for something to do tonight. Everyone's really friendly, too; you'll be sure to get the Canadian experience you're hoping for."

We agree that that sounds like a wonderful idea and thank our waiter (his name is Philip, like the prince) profusely, tip him generously, and make our merry way to the drive-in.

Chapter 8

The drive-in isn't far from the diner: in fact we can see the light of the screens from the parking lot. We paid our ten dollars happily and found ourselves even more happily received into the unique atmosphere that is the drive-in.

What I mean to say is that there is a kind of neighborliness remnant from when drive-ins had their heyday.

"We're not even gonna be able to see the movie," Ro says when we park the jeep between two speakers, ten rows back from the towering, whitewashed screen.

"Hey, can you all not see?" a guy just about our age immediately shouts, as though answering our prayers.

He, one other guy, and three girls are in a truck in front of us, kicking around a soccer ball and eating what looks like sour worms by the gallon.

"No!" we shout back.

The guy holds out a fistful of worms. "Want some candy? You can sit in our van," he says with an impish laugh.

As it turns out, the truck does not even belong to the guy who invited us, it belongs to the girls.

"Came over with sour worms and puppy dog eyes," one of the girls laughs when we find out the fact of the matter. The movie is about to begin and we're all crawling into the blanket pile in the truck-bed.

"Couldn't say no!" another adds.

"So we better hope that this truck bed can really hold as much weight as the commercials say."

I can't help but bounce experimentally. Everyone gives me a look. "Nice shocks," I say.

"So," the guy who invited us over asks hesitantly. He glances up at the movie screen, which has just blasted the omen "COMING SOON" in white and green. He knows he is running out of time. "What's with the legs?"

For a moment, I am confused. Legs ... what about 'em? Yeah, my calves are hecka rad but ... "Huh?"

I look down at my palms, which are flat down on my thighs. My pale, freckled hands strike an almost terrifying, Frankenstein like contrast against my Shimmer Dayz: IT STAYZ 2000 shellacked legs.

"Oh," I say, feeling my equally pale and, as of yet, un-tanned face go red. "Well you see--"

I had been prepared to explain the Irish dancing thing when Ro suddenly cuts me off.

"The goal," she is quoting me.

I have to stop her. I throw a sugar-y hand out to cover her mouth, which she immediately wrestles away and pins, laughing.

I can't stop her.

"The goal is cigarette legs," Ro finishes, giggling like crazy.

"FOLKS YOU HAVE NEVER SEEN ANYTHING LIKE THIS BEFORE!" the speaker in the truck booms.

Blank faces stare. Blank faces squint.

"Well, as you see," I say. Ro begins to laugh uncontrollably. I kick her with one of my Shimmer Dayz beauties. "We're Irish dancers. And so we're up onstage and the main thing we want to be noticed is our legs."

I am punching Róisín in the shoulder repeatedly as I try to explain this clinically. I know I have to get to the part they really want to know. "So if you're pale, like me, it's become custom to tan. And I've started to call them cigarette legs because we wear white socks. So when you've got orange legs and white socks, it looks like a cigarette."

"That's her goal," Róisín says, mock serious.

"I don't condone smoking," is the only thing I can think to say. These people are thinking that we are crazier by the second. Or that I'm crazier, at the very least (granted Róisín is *still* laughing uncontrollably). "We are athletes, after all."

These people are very confused. Very.

"But what about--" one of the girls begins.

"I just haven't gotten to the rest of me yet," I explain lamely. "My legs are the most important part."

Five "oh"s sound from around the truck bed. Then one of the girls shrugs. "Hey, you got it, flaunt it."

"Do it for the sport, man," another says.

"Get your head in the game!"

"GO WILDCATS!" we all shriek at once.

And just like that, we're bonded by the power of the drive-in, sour worms, and HSM once again.

It's a good enough movie for a summer night: some Will Ferrell flick with lines Róisín and I will probably be quoting in text messages for years to come. But we have had enough sugar to last us a lifetime and our bodies, so used to peanut butter and green beans, aren't fit to handle it. Fifteen minutes in and I find myself yawning and notice that Róisín is doing the same.

Will Ferrell does a great impression of a trout (this has nothing to do with the film, I don't think) and that's when I fall asleep.

I wake up to my face being smashed into what feels and smells remarkably like a giant Nike.

"What the--" I open my eyes and sit up abruptly, expecting to see that the movie has ended and our new friends are waiting impatiently for us to make ourselves scarce.

What I actually see is the highway flying by. I look down; I had smashed my face on a spare tire. To my left Róisín is still sleeping soundly, snuggled into a sleeping bag and cuddled around the tub of sour worms as if it were a teddy.

"Ro-SHEEN!" My voice breaks off in a cracked screech, tumbling out of the truck bed and into the cacophony of engines and car horns.

I feel the panic bubbling in my chest as we hit a bump and I am jolted two hops closer to the tailgate.

I claw my way back up and begin shaking my best friend by the legs.

"Hmm?" Róisín mumbles sleepily. Her brow furrows as she slowly comes into awareness.

I am currently gasping for air, the panic arriving now that she is awake.

She opens her eyes just as a police car goes flying by.

"What the hell?" she asks as calmly as one might ask, "Will you pass the salt?"

"Róisín," I whisper desperately. "We're on the highway. How do we *not* be on the highway, Ro? Are we being kidnapped? Is this *Taken*? My dad doesn't have any particular set of skills-- what are you *doing?!*"

Róisín is wriggling out of the sleeping bag and crawling up towards the cab of the truck.

"Hey!" she shouts, slamming a balled up fist against the window. "Hey!"

Suddenly the face of one of the girls from the drive-in appears in the dark window. Her eyes go wide and she mouths what looks like string of expletives.

With great effort, she yanks the window open. "What the hell?" she says, not at all with Róisín's calm.

"No, you!" I shout combatively.

The girl gives me an annoyed look. "Hey, now that's a bit rude!"

I scowl and take a deep breath of gritty, highway air, prepared to release the fury of twenty treble jigs on her soul when she shoves a hand through the tiny window and shouts at me, "Pull over!"

This causes me to scowl and her to shriek. Neither of us knows which way is up, it seems. She pulls her head inside the cab of the truck and shouts, "Oh my gosh SUSAN PULL OVER FOR GOODNESS SAKE."

The truck pulls off to the breakdown lane in a spray of gravel and sand, making me and Róisín cry out, throwing ourselves flat in the truck bed.

When the truck finally grinds to a halt, we lift ourselves up with shaking arms and legs to scramble over the edge of truck.

"Why are you here?" Susan shakes a balled up fist.

"Why did you kidnap us?" I shoot back.

Susan widens her eyes at her friend and stamps a foot. In the dimness of the night and flashing headlights of the cars passing by, Susan looks positively insane and like a potential kidnapper to boot. "We didn't kidnap you! We just ... I don't know ... *forgot* about you!"

"Well that's a bit rude," I can't stop myself from saying.

"Elodie!" Ro chides desperately.

"Sorry." I shrug. "So ... can you bring us back?"

Susan shakes her head. "We've been driving for *two hours.*"

There's silence. Then a small voice from inside the cab. "There's a gas station over there..."

Chapter 9

They have just ditched us.

"The off-ramp is right … there-ish," Not-Susan had said, jabbing a finger at vague, glowing sign that seemed ages off.

"Well, that shatters my All-Canadians-Are-Nice illusion," I grump as we trudge.

"How are we gonna get to the venue?" Róisín says, rubbing the bridge of her nose.

"Uh, we find some wild horse, rope 'em, ride 'em, and sail into the wild blue yonder," I say sleepily.

I should be panicked but, as usual, amusement comes first and foremost. I laugh through blood before I ever feel the throb of a hard fall's achy pain, and that is how I have always been. It is procrastination to the last level.

Róisín, on the other hand, is practical. She sees a problem and wants to fix it, and usually does. It's probably why she is rarely frustrated. She wants solutions and not silliness. Thus, she is having none of my rope 'em and ride 'em plan.

"Let's go there; we can probably call a cab." Róisín is pointing through the syrupy darkness at a glimmering red, white and blue Esso sign in the distance.

We keep trudging. Well, Ro is trudging, I am doing skip 23s and treble clicks absentmindedly, as I always do. I rub my tongue over my teeth, which still taste of sugar. I think to myself that if Declan saw how many sweets we had consumed, he would probably ask us to quit on the spot on mere principle.

"What, a moose cab?" I grumble.

We look both ways before crossing the deserted road, after which Róisín casts me a withering eye roll. "Are you ever going to stop with the Canada jokes?"

"Are we ever going to get out of Canada?" I volley back, pulling open the gas station door.

There doesn't appear to be anyone inside except a buzzing fridge full of beer and a bin beside the cash register that is overflowing with chocolates of every type imaginable. "Is it stealing if no one's around? What if you eat it in the store?"

Our footsteps are muffled on the plasticky linoleum. I do a couple of trebles, to test the sound. Not a great sound, but not too slippy. I give it a seven out of ten.

Róisín peeks over the counter hopefully.

She frowns. "I don't see a phone."

"Maybe in the bathroom?"

"Ew."

"Not the phone, the cashier!" I take the opportunity to roll my eyes at Róisín and seize it. I notice that there is a door behind the counter that is open a crack. "C'mon."

We quickly make our way in, fumbling for a light as it is more or less pitch black. After a few moments of inching along the wall and banging my shin twice, I finally find a switch. Just as I flip it, the door we came through slams shut.

I shriek, Ro shrieks. It's all very *Scream: The TV Series.*

"What are you two doing back here?" a gruff voice snarls.

Cue more shrieking.

Blocking the door is a red ski-masked, red and white-striped shirted man. As a matter of fact, he looks a lot like--

"Who's asking, Waldo?" Róisín digs her nails into my arm as she says this, without so much as a quaver in her voice. I actually have the nerve to laugh.

"Quit your laughin'!" The voice is just as gruff, but with a bit of an offended hitch this time.

"But did you look at yourself when you got dressed? Did you think that because you dressed as Waldo you could rob this store and then people would go, 'Oops, where'd he go?!'" I'm on a roll here.

I am ready to keep going when he strides forward and grabs each of us by an arm. Tight.

"Listen here," he hisses. "I'm gonna be doing the talking, you understand?"

We nod vigorously.

"I'm taking the money and I'm taking you two with me. I ain't gonna have some teenyboppers mess this up for me," he growls. He shoves us in the corner so he can sweep his scattered loot into an old laundry bag.

Ro's eyes widen, clearly saying, "*Run.*"

And I know that should be the only thought on my mind as well but ... I have an idea.

"Where are we going?" I ask curiously.

"Why would I tell you where we're going? Aren't you my hostages?" He's asking me the questions, so I sense that he has not done this before.

"But, like, if you're just gonna let us go after why does it matter if we know? At least we can enjoy the trip together, have something to look forward to, maybe?" I try to force the shake out of my voice and fill it with unsure sweetness instead.

"To Toronto."

"Perfect!" I squeal, grabbing Róisín's hand.

Waldo spins around quickly. "Why?"

I try to force a more somber look on my face: the look of a girl who has now been kidnapped twice in one evening. "It's just we've never seen Toronto. Gotta look on the bright side, right?"

Waldo says nothing, just shakes his head.

"Shall we go?" I chirp.

"Uh, sure," Waldo really was not planning to meet a couple of bossy hostages. "But first ..."

He reaches clumsily for a Scotch tape dispenser on a desk behind him. He knocks over a mug full of pens and a stack of papers and curses.

"Seriously?" Róisín mutters, rolling her eyes.

He opens his mouth in protest.

"Oh *whatever,*" Róisín says. The unsaid, "*If you weren't our only way to get to this competition, so help me*" as clear to me in that exasperated sigh as if she had shouted at him.

She thrusts out her wrists and I follow suit.

"So," I say conversationally as he struggles to get the tape to extend more than two inches without sticking to itself. "What's the weather like in Toronto this time of year? I'm thinking of a timeshare."

He manages one loop around my hands and moves onto Róisín. "Do you ever shut up?" he says.

"No," Róisín replies immediately.

"This is gonna be one hell of a road trip," he mutters, finally taping my wrist to Róisín's.

"Road trip to the cottage," I say automatically, giggling a little.

Ro glares.

He glances down at the now empty roll of tape as though he is regretting not taping my mouth shut.

I force myself to stop laughing in my kidnapper's face and to frown again; one hell of a road trip indeed.

Chapter 10

My hands are getting itchy under the tape. I could easily snap through it, or even slide through the loop on account of my sweat, but I don't want to insult our kidnapper/taxi-driver-unawares only fifteen minutes into a three hour journey; I think I've done enough of that already.

"So, how's the burglary business these days?" I try to lean forward to peek between the front seats to chat with Waldo only to be immediately yanked back into a crumbling haystack and some moldy smelling blankets. I forgot that Ro and I are still attached at the wrist.

"Róisín, gross," I whine. "What even is all this?"

"The bodies of other dead Irish dancers?" she says dully.

I'm starting to feel a little bad about my choice in Ubers for the evening. I mean, obviously it's not ideal, but I do wish Ro would give me some credit; we had a person in the flesh that was going to Toronto and that was just the place we needed to go! I'd be *stupid* to turn down a lift.

I try once again to chat to Waldo, this time without disturbing Róisín.

"So," I say a little louder. "What got you into burglary?"

"This isn't my usual business," Waldo finally responds, peeling off his mask with one hand. Two fidgeting blue eyes peer back at me through the rear-view mirror. "I'm in the shipping business. I transport cattle that's been won in auctions. But ladies don't like it when you smell like a cow all the time." Waldo looks at me woefully. "Do they?"

"Um," I scramble for an answer, suddenly very interested in the tape on my wrist. "Well, I suppose it's an acquired smell and --"

"My lady left me," Waldo cuts in. His voice trembles, causing Róisín's upper lip to curl in disgust. As if being kidnapped wasn't bad enough; now our kidnapper is going to start *crying*? I don't know how much longer Róisín is going to last before she kicks open the back of this moving van and hurls us out onto the pavement, 90 miles-per-hour be damned.

"She left me and I gotta win her back," he sniffs. "So I was on a long haul last week and listening to the radio. Then that lady with the sad songs was on and I called in. I told her what Sally and I were going through and she told me I should do something spontaneous and bold to show her that I can earn her love. And well, here we are."

"So are you telling me," Róisín says in an even, cold voice. "That we've been kidnapped because fricken Delilah told you to rob a store?"

"What's wrong with Delilah?" Waldo says in a wounded tone.

"To be fair I don't think Delilah meant robbery," I cut in weakly. "She probably meant like, some chocolate or a hot air balloon ride."

"Well it was up to interpretation," Waldo says. "My lady said she always had a thing for Bonnie and Clyde and … Why would I get a hot air balloon?"

"Because, you egg, you're--" I throw my hands (plus one of Róisín's) up in the air. "Forget it. Can we just listen to the radio?"

"I don't think you should really be making demands?" Waldo asks because, once again, he's really not sure. Still, he turns on the radio on.

"Hi, good evening! You've called the Delilah Show--"

Róisín shrieks and stamps a foot. This plan is getting better by the minute.

Chapter 11

What I hadn't really thought of was how we are going to escape. Feeling anxious, I put a gentle hand on my dear, sweet, loving, understanding friend's knee.

"Ro-shee," I start to say.

"I know, you walnut," she says through gritted teeth.

You know how I said before that I felt a little bad about my choice of transportation? Well, let's just say that, for the rest of my life, whenever Róisín comes to visit me I'm going to have to fly her first class and get out the nice sheets.

"I'll think of something." I pat her on the knee, trying not to feel insulted by the walnut comment.

It's another mind numbing two hours of bouncing around in itchy hay (which is making my tan flake horribly) and trying to get Róisín to play I-Spy. "I spy with my little eye something red ..."

"Declan's face, as he's screaming at us," Ro mumbles. She yanks her hand away from mine, ripping the pathetic handcuffs apart. She rubs her wrist ruefully, humming Plaxty Davis under her breath as she taps out her steps with her fingers.

"Good idea," I say. "We passed a sign for Toronto City not long ago. I'd say it's about time we start mentally preparing ourselves for the competition."

With that, I hop up to my knees and pop myself over the back of the front seat. I dangle my arms and fiddle with the seatbelts.

"Um, there's an ish," I say. I attempt a look of awkward innocence, biting my lip and crinkling my forward. I check the rearview mirror for Róisín's reaction. Her stare is annoyed as ever. I have to make this good.

"I have to use the bathroom," I say.

"Hold it," he growls.

I watch the tiny cardboard pine tree that is hanging from air vent sway once, twice, three times. My time has come.

I swallow roughly and reply petulantly, "I can't. It's kind of an emergency."

"Well that's just not my pro--"

"Like a *female* emergency!" I cut in.

Waldo's mouth hangs open. Róisín claps her hand to her mouth in a surprised giggle.

"Have you ever seen *Carrie*?" I say.

Waldo swallows and grips the steering wheel a bit tighter. "If it's the end of the world, we'll find a place to stop."

"Not the end of the world," I correct cheekily. "A bloody catastrophe."

Waldo leans forward and I watch the needle of the speedometer inch a bit farther to the right.

I stifle a grin and flop back down beside Róisín, offering her a wink. She shakes her head and sticks out her tongue. If I were really going to have my period at a major, she would have never heard the end of my groaning about the unfairness and cruelty of the world.

It's hardly ten minutes before we catch sight of a Tim Horton's and I whimper in the most pitiful fashion.

"Oh," I hiss in pain. "The cramps ..."

He turns so quickly that we nearly roll, rather than drive, into the parking lot.

The second he opens the door we dash inside to the bathroom.

I lock myself in a stall immediately. I mean, I really do have to pee.

"Elodie!"

"I'm sorry, we were in there ages!"

I hear the click of the stall beside me. Sometimes I think Róisín just likes to shout at me.

A few moments later, we have convened by the sink. As we elbow each other sleepily to fight for the soap, the bathroom door opens and neither of us takes any notice until a man's voice says, "We ain't got all day, girls, um, grandma's ... waiting and uh ... dying."

I jerk my body around so suddenly that I scrape my still soapy wrists on the faucet.

"Ro-shee," I find the words cracking from my throat before I can stop them. I have a sudden urge to grab the sleeve of her jacket, something I used to do when we were little beginners, back when Declan shouting at us would bring me to tears.

For the first time, I don't know what to do. Waldo is standing there, looking as nervous and unsure as ever but this time he is blocking the door. For the first time, I am actually a little scared. I suddenly remember that we are two girls alone in a different country. While yesterday morning I had felt so confident, my "Muscles & Mascara" tank top now feels idiotic; I've literally talked us into the clutches of a kidnapper, stupidly thinking that I could talk us out of it in the end. I feel desperate tears flooding my eyes and an old, familiar panic clutching at my lungs.

Just then, I feel a sweaty, strong hand clasp around my forearm and I am being not dragged but positively *whipped* out of the bathroom. Ro uses the force of three times a week, forty-five minute long, core workouts to hold her ground as she kicks Waldo in the shin harder than she has ever kicked through a heel click in her life.

Waldo falls to the ground, grasping blindly at the air and likely seeing stars. I know the last time Róisín accidentally kicked herself in the ankle while wearing hardshoes that she couldn't even speak for five full minutes, that's how badly it hurt. Through it all, Róisín is screaming. I know that it's Róisín but I hardly recognize the voice; I don't think I've ever heard Róisín scream in my entire life.

"We've been kidnapped! Someone call the cops! This guy has kidnapped us!"

She drags us to the front of the restaurant and runs behind the busy counter, still screaming. One of the clerks must have misunderstood Róisín because she puts her hands up defensively and gasps, "Sorry, do you want Timbits?" but Róisín points at Waldo, still scuttling on the ground in pain by the bathroom.

Even in her fear, Róisín manages to be patient. "No, *he* kidnapped *us!* Call the cops, *please!*"

The entire restaurant of coffee sipping people is wide-eyed and fearful, not aware that Waldo is almost entirely incompetent as a criminal. They know that someone should do something, but no one wants to be the one to do it.

"Someone, catch him!" shouts a lady by the door. She is still holding her doughnut close to her mouth, as if she hopes that if she ignores the situation by going on eating, the situation will disappear.

"Hi, we have an emergency at the Tim Horton's on Front Street, we have two girls who just escaped a kidnapping and the man is still here-- oh no! No! He's gone!" The cashier is frantic.

Waldo stumbles, limping out of the restaurant and into his truck. The second cashier finally springs to action, demonstrating impressive speed, but she isn't quick enough; in mere moments, Waldo has reversed into a handicapped parking sign and roared down the formerly silent street. He leaves road dust and stunned diners in his wake.

It takes ten minutes for the police to show up. In that time, we have been plied with iced coffee and maple doughnuts and sat down at a long counter down by the window. We have been asked "are you sure you're okay?" and "what happened?" so many times and in so many different inflections that I am beginning to wonder if I understand what the words mean at all.

There are four cops present at the "scene of the crime", as it is now being called, and they can hardly hide their excitement. This is clearly the biggest thing that has happened in their little town for ages and the bunch of them are like hummingbirds buzzing off sugar, bopping from one end of the restaurant to the other, gathering statements.

Now that the fear is gone, I am impatiently checking the time. The same thought keeps prancing back and forth: *"You're never gonna make it on time."*

I glance up at a clock that says 9:30. An hour past check-in.

"Excuse me," Róisín says impatiently, tapping the shoulder of the policeman nearest us. He is speaking with the running-cashier.

"And how close were you?" he says excitedly.

"I could smell him," she replies.

"What like?"

"Kind of like, well ... the fair? And not like fried foods and cotton candy, like the 4H tent."

"OH MY GOD," I half scream, half growl through gritted teeth. I grip the counter and mime slamming my head against it.

"Elodie," Róisín grabs me by the shoulders and shakes me. "Do you have any ideas?"

"My last few ideas could've gotten us killed," I remind her.

I glance up at the clock again. With every minute that passes, I imagine the time we are losing. The hand whirs ever so slowly around. With that minute, I lost time to put on false eyelashes. With the next minute, I am going to miss finding a spot in the practice room.

"Hey, Dominic, check it out! The news is here!" one young policeman shouts, literally jumping on the spot for joy.

Róisín grabs my wrists and says in a quiet voice, "Please, El. Think of something. This might be my last major. I probably have to retire after this Worlds and well, that's fine but ..."

Like whenever something unexpected shocks me, I feel as though all the hot, lava-like fear in my body has come erupting from some deep crevice in my heart, suddenly flooding my veins, making the blood rush to my ears.

"What? Ro, why didn't you tell me? Why? If you quit ..." my voice twists off in that tiny way and I beg myself not to cry. I stroke the dusty leaves of a fake potted plant that is on the table in front of me, petting it as if it is a strange puppy that could bring me comfort.

I don't know why I am so upset, exactly. Róisín loves dancing but she loves it because she is good at it, not because she needs it. I have always known that Róisín would quit someday, and someday soon, when "real" life got in the way. But I didn't think about it. And now that Róisín has said it, it feels real and I can't believe how much it hurts.

"We're still gonna be best friends," Róisín says, squeezing my hand. She laughs and I can hear the tears in her voice as well, though there is no evidence of them otherwise. "I'm gonna be the first Irish dancer specialized physical therapist, remember?"

I chuckle weakly and wipe away an errant tear with my free hand.

"Yeah, only because I'm so stupid and get hurt all the time."

"No, because I'm going to keep you from getting injured," Róisín corrects me. Then she smiles.

"You're the dancer, El," she says.

I shake my head and quote our first teacher, Miss Orla, who had a particular exasperated fondness for my never-ceasing (but always out of time) hop 123s. "Just a bit of grá in my heart."

"And you're gonna use that love to lead the céilí at my funeral, which will be soon, because Declan is going to murder us if we don't make it on-time to figures."

I laugh again, for real this time, and wipe away the lingering tears in my eyes. "Okay, plan!"

The coffee shop has more or less gone back to business, with 20-something construction workers wiping sleep and sawdust out of their eyes and bored receptionists filing in for the office coffee run. Forget the *Sixty Minutes: Kidnapping Special;* our five minutes of fame has come and gone.

My eyes fall on an empty squad car. The doors are wide open.

"Ro-shee, do you ever wonder how many action/adventure movies might be going on around you?" I say with measured excitement. I leap up and stride towards the door.

She is apprehensive. "What? No …"

The door closes behind us with a jingling of bells.

"Well maybe this is our own action/adventure movie! We need to take matters into our own hands …"

I gesture grandly at the squad car and raise my eyebrows suggestively. "Well?!"

Róisín stares at me. And she stares at me. She squints at me. Then her jaw drops open.

"Elodie Kennedy!" she snaps sternly.

I jump back in surprise and can't help but laugh. "What?"

"After all we've been through today! First, you convince someone to kidnap us and now this. For goodness sake, girl, I better not quit or you're going to end up in *jail* for one of these grand schemes."

Róisín grabs me by the scruff of my shirt like a puppy and I am full on laughing. Okay, so maybe that was my worst idea today, but at least in comparison the Waldo situation looks tame!

I wiggle out of Róisín's grip just as she has reached a policeman. I have a sudden fear that Ro is going to turn me in, just to teach me a lesson. I'm about to plead my case when she starts talking.

"I'm sorry," she says loudly, interrupting his conversation with a news reporter. She is as sorry as she is pleased with me. "We need you to take us to Memorial Hall. Now."

I do skip 23s to car.

"Road trip to the cottage!" I squeal.

Chapter 12

My heart is pounding.

The venue is absolutely packed. My eyes are blinded by glitter and I can hardly take a breath for the thin mist of hairspray that clings to the air. Róisín and I had hardly thanked the officer properly before leaping out of car and running.

I felt like a squirrel in the middle of the road caught between two equally terrible options; had we not made it, I would've rather died, but now that we're here, there's a real possibility Declan will put us in the grave himself. We are unsure whether we should wait for someone to find us or run. We decide to keep running.

We weave our way through vendors pawning gleaming tiaras and leap over little girls gluing socks to their shins. We shove through the clumps of dancers in velvety dresses and try not to look reproachful mothers in the eye.

We are barreling towards a door marked "BALLROOM A" when someone shouts, "Wristbands!"

We screech to a halt.

My hands are flat on the door and it takes genuine willpower not to ignore this bored dance dad, some man who can't tell a hornpipe from a heavy jig and is only running the check-in table because he was strong-armed into it by his child or wife.

I whirl around and rush to the table. "Elodie Kennedy, Rooney Academy!" I shove my right hand in front of his face and wiggle it impatiently.

"Please," I beg. "Hurry, our figure has to be any minute!"

"Figures," he sputters and begins fumbling with a variety of clipboards. He glances up at Róisín, who looks ready to snatch any one of the check-in lists out of his hands if the opportunity presents itself.

"And who are you?" he asks, sounding flustered.

"Róisín!" A shout comes from across the crowded atrium. "Elodie!"

Suddenly, one dark, curly, tiara-encrusted wig stands out to me from the mob of other dark, curly, tiara-encrusted wigs. The wig is attached to Kasey, who is leaping into the air and waving frantically, eyes wide. She gracelessly shoves a few pre-teen dancers, who are drinking milkshakes and paying zero attention to the world around them, and she runs to us.

Kasey is dressed in our team costume, soft shoes, and is wearing a look of fury that is entirely out of place when coupled with her perfect Cupid's bow lipstick and fluffy falsies. I realize the worst a moment before she opens her mouth.

"We had to do our figure with you!" she confirms my fear. I taste remorse on my tongue and it tastes a lot like sour worms and hay dust.

Kasey is still glaring at us. "We had to dance it with two of the intermediates! Where were you guys? How could you?"

"It's such a long story," Ro shakes her head. "We're so sorry. We can't begin to say how sorry we are."

"Please help us get into the ballroom for solos?" I am surprised at the tremble in my voice and bite my lip. "We'll explain everything, Kase. I promise."

Kasey gives me a long stare, hands on her hips, but she seems to soften. Or, at least, the furious crease between her eyebrows does.

"God, fine. I'm still mad," she clarifies. I nod in understanding. "And worried? I think I'm worried about you guys?"

She holds her hand out to the man at the check-in desk. "Róisín O'Shea and Elodie Kennedy. Wristbands." She wiggles her fingers impatiently until the man deposits them in her hand. She rolls her eyes. "Thanks."

We stride into the ballroom and Kasey has cooled down enough to start making observations. "Guys, where are your dresses? And shoes? And your ... *everything?*"

I grab her by the arm and steer her in the direction of our teammates. "About that; we have none."

"No shoes?" she squints at me and nods. "Okay, we can fix that."

"No," Róisín corrects her. "No nothing. This is it. Us. We are all we have."

Kasey blinks once. Twice. She wants to ask.

"Shh, shh," a whisper comes crackling over the microphone. "Girls 18 and under, please report side stage."

This is the age group before Róisín and me. We don't have time to tell our story yet.

"CAT!" Kasey roars suddenly, making about seven different girls with the same name embroidered on their jackets peer in her direction, one of whom is positioned in a huddle of girls twenty feet away from us. That huddle of girls happens to be our teammates. Imagine eleven baby birds simultaneously opening their mouths to be fed; that is the sight that greets us. Of course, these little chickens want the hot goss on why Róisín and I have bailed on our most important competition of the year. Kasey has decided that she won't allow it.

"Ro and El need make-up, shoes, socks, and teams outfits. Fifteen minutes, that's it." Kasey is sharp and final and the girls immediately begin shouting what they have.

They swarm us.

"I'll do Ro's make-up."

"I've got El!"

"I can fix hair ... Elodie, why do you have *hay* in yours?"

"Here, have my socks!" Rachel is in the process of peeling her socks off her own feet before Kat protests, "Guh-ross, Rach! I have spares in my bag!"

In fifteen short minutes, I have had Quirk apologize to me ten times for burning my ears just as many times with a hair straightener, Emily has accidentally poked me in the eye with a bobby pin, and Kat has force-fed me several peanuts, all while Cat has stood by and snapchatted the ordeal.

Anya quirks her eyebrow at me as she applies glue to a set of eyelashes; Anya always helps me put on my lashes. The normalcy of it, suddenly, in this day, makes me feel like things are on the path to going right again.

"I'm gonna try to not glue your eyes shut this time," she says.

"If you didn't, I'd be worried. It's practically good luck at this stage," I laugh.

She puts on the lashes and, for a moment, as always, my eyes seem stuck together.

We laugh as Anya tries to help me unstick them. "Well, as Declan would say, 'You should know your steps well enough to dance them in the dark, my dear'".

Anya's Declan impression is spot on. I laugh my eyes unstuck and launch myself into her arms. Anya isn't one for hugs, but I love her and can't help it.

"Declan is going to be *so mad* at me," I whisper into her shoulder. "So would you mind giving me a speech?"

Anya gives me a little pat on the arm and pushes me away. Grinning she says, "Now get out there and do what you've trained to do. Show them that you are Elodie Kennedy: not my niece, not my dancer, not any dancer at all. You are *the* dancer and the only dancer that they want to watch today. Love every second of it. Not to win it, just to live it."

My heart beats twice. It crawls towards my throat. I shove it down with a laugh.

"Anya, if Declan ever heard you I think he might hire you. He always says he's sick of talking; you could just do it for him."

"Shh, shh, shh, quiet in the hall please," a voice chirps over the microphone again. "Would Girls and Boys 19-20 please report side stage?"

"That's us!" I squeak. "Can I have the dress?"

Anya hands me her teams dress. It is black, with a high collar, and long sleeves. There is no embroidery, no sequins, no nothing. I shimmy into it.

Anya nods and winks. "Good woman."

Róisín has taken a bit longer getting ready; the girls had to borrow make-up off one of the only other black dancers, making us all tut over the lack of variety in palettes. Róisín has barely put her second arm through the sleeve of her dress before I grab it and make us sprint to the stage.

Standing side-stage always reminds me of the way I would press my nose up against the glass barrier at the zoo when I was a little girl. The seven inches of glass would disappear and I would be eye-to-eye with smiling cheetahs and silky-maned lions. They would look so sweet and soft, tiptoeing gently around the carefully constructed playhouses, seeming to be animal actors in a pretend animal kingdom. But reality would always bleed through that seven-inch glass, which was just smudged enough by tiny dirt-covered hands like mine to draw your attention to the charade; that thick, smudged glass served as a reminder that these were not friendly house cats looking to make friends, but predators searching for prey.

Dancers side-stage aren't any different. Despite the soft velvet and watery silks and the schoolgirl-like socks, the Sunday school curls the lipstick hellos and the good luck goodbyes, no girl is here to lose.

Some girls are fierce, bordering on vicious: "I hear the stage is really slippy," they will say with a frown. "I don't know if I'll go full out."

Your heart immediately skips. You scuff your toe on the ground and try not to be too obvious when glancing at the stage. A girl who is so high on her toes that she looks like the porcelain ballerina inside your jewelry box, just as pin-straight but ten times as fast as she twirls around her competition. You look back around and the other girl is already gone, frowning to the next girl in line. You straighten your number and stand up a bit taller. You will not be intimidated.

Some girls are coy: "Elodie, love! I haven't seen ye in an age! Ah God, no I haven't a *hope* of recalling, I doubt I'll even remember all my steps. Now what about ye, honestly? Do you think you'll qualify? I know you've been trying at it for the last few years."

You shrug and smile shyly, avoiding the question. "Ah, you'll be great! Don't worry, just have fun!"

And some girls are silent; I look at Róisín. She does not practice her steps. She waves at a few girls she knows and exchanges friendly but brief conversation before turning back around to face the stage. She watches it, not the others; she knows it is the stage she has to kill, not her competitors.

I never know how to be. Right now, my heart is in my throat and somehow the ringing in my ears manages to drown out the din of accordion and my toes have gone numb in Anya's soft shoes, which are two sizes smaller than my size, which are two sizes smaller than my street shoes. The only way I manage a semblance of calm is by crossing my feet tightly in fifth position, closing my eyes, and imagining my steps in time with the music. I try to slow my heart to the beat of the metronome.

"Two thirty-four?" an impatient voice breaks through my reverie.

My eyes snap open to reveal a face that is too close to my own. An elderly TCRG who has not the time for dilly-dallying, she rolls her eyes, brushes some (probably) visible dust off my shoulder and says, "Off you go, dear."

My legs go stiff and wobbly at the same time as I make my way to my position before the judges. A flash of memory strikes me and I remember a cartoon that I watched as a child that starred a clay cowboy.

One of the judges holds up his hand as he checks over some last minute details, stalling the start of our round. My mind is racing. (Am I dancing reel right now? I don't know. What was that silly green cowboy's name?)

"Good luck," the girl beside me smiles. I don't know her but she smiles with only her top six teeth and that makes me trust her.

"Gumby," I mumble. My eyes widen in embarrassment and exultation. (Gumby, that was his name!) "I mean, good luck!"

Except the "luck" bit is cut off by the accordion coughing back to life. A few beats, then I am pointing my toe without even realizing it, the instrument is humming away and I am gone.

I don't realize that I have been dancing until halfway through the left foot of my first step. I am in front of the judge to the far left when she pauses her scratching away at her scoring sheet and looks up. At me.

Warmth fills my chest, like the feeling of sun on your skin after four months of winter, and I grin at that judge. And she grins right back: six top teeth.

It is in that moment that I realize that I have not been dancing at all-- I have been flying.

Cliché though it is, it's the truth. My leaps feel as though they were manufactured by the wind as I am lifted off the floor and above the crowd. My feet barely have the chance to touch the floor as I flutter from trick to trick, twirling from corner to corner of the stage like a bird showing off its lovely feathers. For the first time in my dancing career, I am not wildly searching the faces of the audience for evidence of my failure.

I am so happy dancing my next two rounds, I actually wonder mid treble jig if perhaps I am *too happy,* maybe smiling *too much*. The thought is so preposterous that I actually let a little giggle slip loose as I flawlessly complete a particularly difficult rhythmic piece, with lots of varying treble speeds and strange placements. The judge nods at me.

When the bell rings for us to bow, I don't want to leave the stage. Normally, I can't run away quick enough to gasp air back into my lungs in private. Today, as my chest heaves and sweat prickles at my neck, I can't stop looking back at the floor where I have just danced. I nearly expect to see a tiny brick being laid into the corner of the rented floor, one that reads, "On this floor Elodie Kennedy ceased to dance and became a dancer."

Like a haggard wave, my group of dancers staggers off stage in a jagged line as a new group swells past us. A pain like white-hot sewing needles jabbing delicately into my bones has begun pinching at my toes and I limp ever so slightly as I wander under the bright lights of the ballroom. I am about to collapse into the nearest available chair, 90% sure that it is not currently occupied by a small child masquerading as a pile of clothes, when I notice a pack of wild girls charging me.

They are frenzied rhinos, heads down with tiaras pointed like horns. I forget my pain for a moment and jump into the air gleefully, ready to land in a tumble with my giggling tribe. Instead, I find myself caught in a firm grip, a hand on either one of my forearms.

"What was that?" a familiar voice asks.

My blood, which has barely had the time to warm up in the course of three short rounds, freezes. I slowly pivot, literally tiptoeing around Mr. Declan, for fear of setting off the fireworks.

I shrug my shoulders up to my ears and smile. This pose has always caused my parents to say, "Don't get all cute", only ever indicating to me that it was, in fact, quite cute. This of course makes him furious.

"Elodie Ann Kennedy, I don't think you understand what you've put me through today!" he thunders. The shock of him shouting *at me*, rather than my dancing or my laziness or my giggling, nearly strikes tears in my eyes. I look around wildly, hoping I can focus on something else and avoid crying. There is an announcement going over the loudspeakers. I try to focus on the words but I only hear the feedback of the microphone.

"One of my busiest days of the year and you've gone *missing*. I have a dozen beginners clinging to my legs, judges asking me to do this, that, and the other, and then I have your mother and father calling me frantic because they *don't know where you are.*"

Declan is getting thick with me and so is his accent. "What do ye have to say for that?"

I can't explain to him everything that has happened today except for the elation of those perfect rounds.

"That that was the best I've ever danced," I hazard with a mumble.

The air freezes between us. Then there is a choking-like sound. I peek up through my eyelashes.

Mr. Declan is *laughing*. Full on, face in hands, grinning laughter.

"What?" I can't help but laugh at the sight of him. "Uncle Declan," the name, one I have not called him since I was little, slips out of me. "What!"

He removes his face from his hand and tries to scrub the smile off his face, to no avail. He lunges forward and gives me a half-hug. "That's my girl," he says. His blue eyes are bright as he beams at me.

I remember the Uncle Declan of my childhood, before he became a teacher and was simply my Auntie Laura's husband, the man with the funny accent and the even funnier dancing. As a child there were countless trad sessions turned sleepover. Diddlyi music became a lullaby to me, as I was chased to dreamland by the timed stomp of a foot, yawning accordions, and fluttery fiddles. I would lay in a dark room, on a bed full of coats and other momentarily forgotten little girls, and I'd nearly be asleep, dreaming of fairies and selkies and running through fields for hours but never getting tired, when suddenly I'd hear a shuffle on the floor. Then a step. Then again. Then a shuffle step shuffle step, and again it would go, before the rhythm would change and I would drop out of bed and creep to the door to watch.

Mr. Declan, hardly twenty then, would be dancing sean nós and I was smitten. I did not know why I wanted to dance except that I felt it in my heart first, my toes second, and my head last of all. After a tune or two, Uncle Declan would lend me a wink and a hand and draw me out of the doorway.

Then we would dance.

He taught me my skips and to point my toe and 'Shoe the Donkey'. I never wanted to stop; but I was only small, and even little girls get tired.

"My wee Ellie is going to be my first champ, aren't ya?" He would ask, cuddling me up on his lap when at last I was too sleepy to twirl or hop even once more.

I give my current day Mr. Declan a squeeze just as an announcement comes over the loudspeaker.

"If we could please have quiet in the hall, we will now be announcing all recalls."

I bite my lip and jump in the air, trying not to shriek. Just then, Róisín comes running into view.

"They'reannouncingrecalls!" She runs straight towards me, grabbing both my hands and spinning me in a circle.

"Sit, sit." Mr. Declan shoos us towards chairs. He tries to quell our giggling but he can hardly keep the grin off his own face.

"So," he says suddenly, rearranging his features into a mockery of his typical serious expression. "Care to explain what happened today?"

"Well, we're never camping again." Róisín nods sincerely.

"Always told you it was pointless," he rolls his eyes. "And ...?"

I grab a programme out of his hand and flip through it casually. I like to look at the embarrassing "good luck lovey sweet girl" advertisements some parents buy.

I shrug. "And I'm never getting in a car with a stranger again."

"Well I'd hope-- wait, Elodie--" Mr. Declan stutters.

"And will I never purposely get myself and/or Róisín kidnapped again."

"ELODIE!"

"SHH!" Declan is hushed by a cross looking mother with a brown bob and a salmon Land's End tee shirt. She twists the silver necklace at her neck delicately. "They're about to *start*," she reprimands.

"Excuse me," Mr. Declan begins to sputter.

"Shh," I whisper, still looking down at the programme. "Can't you see they're about to start?"

Mr. Declan tears the programme out of my hand and slumps down in his seat like a sulky child.

But he does not have long to sulk. To the satisfaction of the Dance Mom ™ behind us, it is only seconds later that the MC of the evening takes the stage with a microphone in one hand and clipboard in another. An anticipatory silence drenches the ballroom. It's so heavy; I want to scream out, "Just tell me already!"

I satisfy myself with whispering it through gritted teeth to Mr. Declan and Róisín, digging my fingernails into their kneecaps, which rest on either side of my own.

"We will now be announcing the competitors who have recalled for the North American Open Championships 2016. We ask that there is complete silence in the hall and that you please save your celebrations until all the recalled dancers have been announced. This list will be posted side stage following this announcement. Now, recalled competitors for Girls ages 10-11 …"

The numbers blend after a while. All I need to know is my number. 234. I stare down at the small square of cardstock by my hip and read the number upside down. 234. All they need to do is call out 234.

"227 …"

"Yes!" Róisín gasps quietly, clenching her fist on my thigh.

"Congratulations, pet," says Mr. Declan. He grins and punches her shoulder gently.

"232 … 233 … 237 …"

I blink. I swallow. I hold my number, still upside down, my fingers leaving sweaty imprints. Maybe … I was wrong. Maybe they …

"Now, onto senior ladies 21 and over."

My fist curls around my number, crushing it into a sweaty ball. But I don't let go.

"Congrats, Ro," I say. I feel my mouth turn up in a smile. I twist in my seat and hug her. "You did it."

Róisín's arms go around me. Despite our twenty-four hours of maple syrup and bouncing around in truck trailers, the smell of lavender still clings to her skin. She squeezes me gently and that gentle squeeze is just too much. I feel the tears crawl from inside me to my eyes. But I can't cry here: I can't look the sore loser, can't look so selfish.

"I'm so proud of you," I say in a soft voice. I casually rub my wet eyes on my fist before I sit up. I force my mouth into that numb smile once again. "Want me to watch your set?"

Chapter 13

Róisín dances like the sun refracted through glass, making rainbows on the walls; it is a beautiful science that always leaves everyone with some kind of feeling. She places second and we are all thrilled.

I once read a book that described love as that feeling you get when you wake up in the middle of the night, cold, disoriented, and for some reason thinking about your fourteenth birthday and the way the cheap frosting on your cake tasted too sweet. And you're sad. So sad and the bed feels so big that it's as if you're a little raggedy doll sunken in the middle of it, not able to move unless a kind child breathes life into you again.

Love is the feeling that follows this. When the person lying beside you (who is breathing so easily and softly that you have nearly forgotten their existence) rolls closer to you and slips their arm around you. Elbow under elbows, chin snuggled over shoulder, they press their curled hand to your heart and sigh sweetly as if to say, "*there* you are." And suddenly you are as warm as a summer puddle, you wiggle your fingers and toes and scoot closer to this incredible person, already delighted for their eyes to open for you in the morning

Well, I have never had a person who has made me feel this; who has made the world both smaller and larger for me at the same time. But I have always had dance.

When I have laid in bed at night frozen in terror, unsure of who I was and how I ended up in this world, I rolled over and spotted my dance shoes in a pile by a door. Their leather molded perfectly to me; faded to grey by my little toe, where I leaned too much; chipped on the heels from thousands of clicks; drenched in my sweat and broken in by my blood, my DNA is as much a part of the design as the stitching on the soles. On their own they were just silly-looking shoes. On my own I was just stunned, stumbling Elodie. But together was magic; together we made a dancer. I would see those shoes waiting by the door and I would think of the many lovely things dance had brought me. Friendship, happiness, heartache, pride, courage … I would instantly be enchanted with dreams of success. I would collapse into my pillow so I could wake up, train harder, and put on those shoes and find myself a better dancer than the day before.

Surely that is love?

Chapter 14

Following the parade of champions, I quickly slip out of the ballroom for a breath of fresh air. After a weaving my way through the bugleweed-lined paths the hotel grounds, I retreat from the muggy summer air back into the air-conditioned elements. It isn't long before I realize, however, I have nowhere to go. After all, Róisín and I have no car and no room.

I wander numbly and aimlessly. Girls and boys are running wild up and down the halls in various states of feis wear. Parents and TCs were clinking glasses at the hotel bar. Tiny kids are playing hide-and-seek in the elevators and capture the flag with their wigs. It won't be long before the musicians get an aul session going and the teachers start a céilí in the atrium. In short, the party has begun.

Normally one of my favorite parts of the day, I could not be less interested. Every time I encounter a cheerful dancer, I bounce away like a pinball, wanting to get as far away as possible. I bounce my way up and down stairways until I find a quiet room.

A large room with no chairs and only a dance floor in the middle, there is not a soul to be found. It is the second ballroom. Today, it was the practice room.

For a few moments, I stare at it like an enemy. I want to feel some fury towards everything this room symbolizes. But anger doesn't rise. Slowly, I scuff off my shoes and patter toward the center of the floor.

"Competitor 234," I say quietly, pointing my toe. "Dancing Rodney's Glory at 109."

I am half-heartedly dancing, my steps silent in my sock feet, when from behind me a voice calls gently, "Toes, stamp."

I stumble and turn around. Declan is standing in the doorway with his arms across his chest; how is it that he constantly catching me out? He lifts one hand and twirls his finger in a circle, telling me to go on.

"Toes, stamp! Out 123 and a click and a click …"

Mr. Declan calls out the rest of the dance to me. My breath is gentle. Declan's voice is echoe-y in the big room, but soft. It is calm. I make no mistakes.

I point and bow when I finish and Mr. Declan claps politely. I walk over and collapse at his feet, just as I have a tendency to do at class after I've danced full out and am ready for corrections. I haven't danced full-out, but I am exhausted.

Declan sits beside me. We sit crisscross-apple-sauce, heads bowed. I play with my socks. It is a long time before Declan says, "I would've recalled you, if just to see that on stage for once."

"Thank you." I roll my sock down and pick at the glue on my leg. "Sometimes I think it's not fair."

I can't look at my teacher. What I'm about to say is reprehensible. I can feel the tears welling in my eyes, so hot they might sizzle on my burning cheeks. I force myself to continue speaking. My voice quivers as I go on.

"It's not fair that Róisín doesn't need it and has it. But I need it and I'll never, ever get it."

And with those words, I feel the ground give way beneath my world. I have a vague notion of Declan putting his arms around my shoulders and all the energy slips out of me like water down a drain. The tears fall in earnest against his starchy shirt.

"Why do you need it, Elodie?" he soothes, rubbing my back gently. "Is this just about the deal with your parents and qualifying?"

Visions of myself with a qualifier medal send fresh torrents of tears down my cheeks. Of calling my parents over the phone and telling them I'm going to Worlds. Of Declan cheering my name.

"I wanted to make you all proud," I hiccup.

I then imagine myself receiving my TCRG certificate, doing a skip around the stage with the other newly qualified teachers. Of putting the certificate on the wall, where my college degree would have gone. Of my first class of babies. Of my first student at a feis.

I mumble, "I wanted people to see how much work I put in. That I'm worthy of being a dancer. 'Cause even though I'm not the best, I love it like I am."

Declan gently detaches me from his chest and holds me by the shoulders.

"Hey," he says, giving me a gentle shake. "You don't 'need it', El." He pats the top of my borrowed wig, shoving pins into my scalp. I don't even care. "You've already got it."

Chapter 15

Despite Declan's kind words, I have some trouble bouncing back in the weeks that follows Oireachtas. Between Buzzfeed articles blaring titles like, "Crazy Pageant Girls Get Kidnapped: ON PURPOSE" and the having to explain to dance parents that the photos of myself and Roisin in the back of a cop car aren't as bad as they look, there's lot of grinning and bearing it going on. And if I'm asked, "Didn't your parents teach you not to get into cars with strangers?" one more time, I might implode. I mean, I'm sure you can only imagine the horror of my parents when the full story of mine and Roisin's Oireachtas adventure came out.

That's not to mention my horror over what to do now that it's all over. While Mr. Declan continues to convince me that he supports my pursuit of my TCRG, I am sick with anxious fear over what to do about my parents' ultimatum.

I very quickly realize that I have two options.

A. Rebel. Go for my TCRG despite their disapproval and general lack of support

or

B. Compromise. Find a solution that allowed for me to make my parents and myself happy.

As I was already a dropout, Option A was pretty bleak. So Option B it was.

I hardly sleep, as I dedicate every hour of the day that I'm not dancing to researching a solution that does not involve me returning to my previous course. It comes to me, epiphany-like, two and a half weeks after the Oireachtas.

Ro and I are do flutter knees at class one night.

"I just can't make it as flutter-y as you!" I gripe. I jump into the air and wildly kick my leg for the hundredth time that evening.

"Try squeezing all your quad muscles and focus on that instead of kicking so much," Ro says as she once again perfectly executes the move.

I give her advice a try. Like magic, suddenly my foot is all a-flutter.

"Amazing!" I say, doing it again. "How did you figure that out?"

"All my PT training!" she says. "Best thing I ever did for my dancing."

"And they say you can't study what you love," I joke. And that's when it hits me.

"Oh, Ro," I say, stunned with this revelation. My friend stares at me, her eyebrow quirked. "I know what I'm gonna do."

Róisín grins.

Myself, Mr. Declan, Róisín, and my parents sit down at the Cèilidh Club for drinks one evening to discuss. I had chosen the location, hoping for home field advantage.

"Community ... college?" My mom tries to hide her distaste. My mom is lovely. My mom is kind. My mom is also a PhD.

"What's wrong with it?" I say innocently. I slurp my Shirley Temple.

Mom doesn't want to insult my Uncle Declan, who has no college education, but she also doesn't want to sound like she approves. She is in a pickle, to say the least.

"Jimmy?" she pleads with my dad to help her.

Dad is good with words. Dad doesn't have a PhD but he has two master's, so he might as well.

"Honey, we just had really hoped that if Worlds didn't work out, you would pick up where you left off at URI. Didn't you like URI?" he encourages gently.

"It's fine," I concede. "But I couldn't dance there, not properly. I need to be able to keep dancing. I'm getting my TCRG and that's that. I'm a good teacher. If you saw me teach, you'd know."

I feel a little unsure, speaking so confidently about myself, and it must show because Declan quickly chimes in.

"Elodie is the best teacher I have. She is a talented dancer, and that's important in a teacher, but what's more important is that she has struggled. When her students struggle, she understands because she has been there."

"Basically, I've sucked too," I clarify.

"What she's SAYING," Róisín says loudly, trying to keep this conversation on a positive track. "Is that despite hardship, there's nothing El loves more than dance."

Róisín says it exactly as we rehearsed; we high-five discreetly under the bar.

"And if you want me to go to college, I'll do that; I *like* learning. But on my terms and with a course that will benefit my teaching," I say.

Mom picks up the printout I've put on the bar.

"So a physical therapy *assistant?*" Mom is still sceptical.

"Ro gave me the idea! It's still full-on and four years. Besides, I'm not trying to *be* a PT, I just want to understand how the body works so I can understand my dancer's injuries--"

"And maybe your own--" Declan and Róisín chime together.

"And how to isolate the muscles that give us the most power," I say, each word carefully measured. This time Róisín high-fives me; we really did rehearse very well.

There are some fluttering of papers and sipping of cokes and cider. I push the TCRG syllabus closer to them.

"And don't forget. This counts as education, too; it's hard work. Irish and history and dancing ... It's what I really want. And Mister ... Uncle Declan wants me as a teacher. After all, I've only made two kids cry this year, so that's breaking his record by a long shot."

My father smiles at his brother in-law. "You always said since Ellie could walk that if we got her dancing, she'd never stop. I guess you called it."

Declan laughs. "That's evident."

My dad shuffles the course work papers into a pile. They are now damp from the bar but he folds them gently into his back pocket.

He beams and throws an arm around me. "So I guess we'll have another teacher in the family after all, won't we, El?"

I nod shyly.

"Well, Miss Elodie, how about a dance to celebrate?" My dad smiles and sounds somewhat abashed. "We know you girls wanted to be grown-up, but we missed being with you at the Oireachtas this year."

"And look how well that worked out," Declan mutters to his drink. Mom elbows him in the ribs. The Double Kidnapping of 2016 (Ro and El Edition) is not to be mentioned again until Christmas, at least.

I twirl around on my stool to face Róisín. Mr. Declan has already stood up, rubbing his ribs, and is strolling towards the corner where a dusty tower of speakers lives.

"C'mon." I grab Róisín's arm and leap to the ground. "Together this time."

40044404R00050

Made in the USA
Middletown, DE
01 February 2017